People and Notes

Limited Edition
This Is Copy
No. 299 Of 300
Copies Printed

"All I ever wanted to do was to play the Sousaphone in the Southern Oregon Symphonic Band."

—Cartoon from *Alice's Adventures in Wonderland* (Altemus. Philadelphia. 1900)

People and Notes

Southern Oregon Symphonic Band

And Its Predecessor

The Hillah Temple Shrine Band

Bert Webber - Editor

Reflected Images Publishers

Printed In U.S.A.

Kindly direct all inquiries to the Publisher:

Published by:
Reflected Images Publishers
Division of
WEBB RESEARCH GROUP PUBLISHERS
P.O. Box 314 Medford, OR 97501

Library of Congress Cataloging-in-Publication Data For Librarians:

People and notes : Southern Oregon Symphonic Band and its predecessor the Hillah Temple Shrine band. / Bert Webber, Editor
p. cm.
Includes index.
ISBN 1-878815-06-7
1. Southern Oregon Symphonic Band–History. 2. Hillah Temple Shrine Band–History. 3. Band Music–Oregon–History and criticism.
I. Webber, Bert.
ML 1311.707P46 1994 94-424447
785.8'06'0795–dc20 CIP MN

Table of Contents

On September 27, 1994, Band President Chris Hald issued a Proclamation:

Be It Known That Irving A. "Irv" Mirick is Hereby Proclaimed to Be:

Director Emeritus and Musician Extraordinary.
May Your Retirement From the Bands Be
Without Discord and Unnecessary Accidentals

Irv Mirick was presented with a handsome plaque bearing the inscription: "This Memento is Presented to You by the Members of the Hillah Temple Shrine Band and Southern Oregon Symphonic Band."

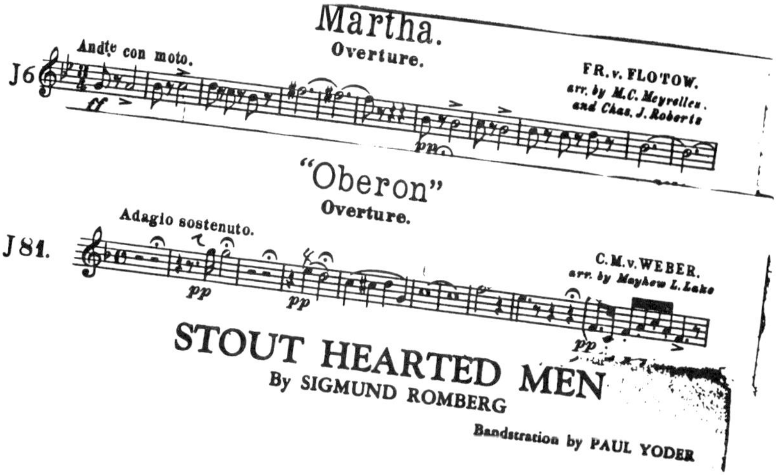

Introduction and Acknowledgements

As a part of becoming a member of the band, an autobiography of each person is requested that specifically relates to the applicant's instrumental musical history. This bio-sketch assists the Director so he learns, more-or-less, what the applicant can do.

For several years, it has been the desire of the Board of Control of the Band that a list of the membership be published. The initial intention was that the list just be a set of copy-machine sheets, but this has evolved to the present book.

The purpose of doing this book is primarily archival. This is because in the past, with the predecessor bands, formal lists of the members have not been located. Knowledge as to who some of these bandsman were becomes lost as the old timers expire. By doing the "list" in recognized book form, every name in the book is now somewhat engraved in granite. This is because this book has computer access International Standard Book Number with copies deposited with the Library of Congress, Washington, D. C.

In Oregon, at least two copies of this book finds their way into the Oregon State Library. One copy is "archival." Others are available for loan to any public and most school libraries in the English speaking world through an established inter-library loan program.

A secondary purpose is so the members will have a "memory book" that in years down the road might become important to their offspring's. This book also is of interest to genealogists because of the dozens of names it contains.

The first publishing idea was pretty Spartan – just pages of names, a little about each person's musical history, and what instruments were involved. The first refinement was to move away from plain sheets with a staple in the corner, to a book. This way the pages could be better kept together. Then it was decided to add a few pictures. At the least, there would be a photograph of the present Director. It was not long before it was realized there are many persons in the Band, with important past-and-present instrumental experiences, who might have pictures. Accordingly, a call went out for photographs.

> Just send what you have. If you were in a band in the junior high school and had a suitable individual picture, send it in. If your present accomplishments are such that you rated a newspaper feature story, send in the picture.

And there were many points midway between school and present where pictures were made that might be suitable. For the most part, all of the pictures submitted are included – but we did eliminate some snapshots that were pretty fuzzy and would not reasonably reproduce.

So this book is the "list" the Board of Control always wanted.

* * *

The editor wishes to acknowledge the help of the members of the Board of Control, especially Band President Chris Hald, and Director John Drysdale. Between them, these two gentlemen knew everybody in the present Band. Hald, from the "good old days" of the early Shrine Band and Drysdale, as the present Director, knows all of the newer members. Some others, who are old timers, offered reflections. These included but were not limited to Irv Mirick, Bill Laurine (who has been in the band since 1947), Duke McQueen and Randy Hugdahl and Harry Kannasto.

We returned the autobiography sheets for updating, then returned some of the updates for more information. A number of the members were telephoned for refinements. Of course, the amount of information on the members varies widely. This is because some have been involved with instrumental music for more than half-a-century. Others are relatively newcomers – the youngest age is 25 – and some had early instrumental musical experiences then abandoned their horns for nearly a lifetime of busy employment in other fields. (The richness of today's Band is enhanced by a number of these senior citizens who have joined the Southern Oregon Symphonic Band.) And some of the members just had more to say than others. The completion of the bio-sketch sheet was not mandatory. Should any Band-person decline to have his bio-sketch included here, he could say so without prejudice.

This book has been a fun project within the band community. The putting it together was handled by the editor on a volunteer basis being sandwiched between his other publishing projects. As many of the photographs submitted were in various shades of color, some badly faded with age, Tuba player Preston Mitchell, a Commercial Photographer, made copies in black and white for publication.

The editor appreciates the interest and help of the members named here, and of all the folks in the Band for their individual efforts to make this the good book that it has become.

Bert Webber (Baritone Horn)
Editor and Publisher
Central Point, Oregon.
Fall 1994

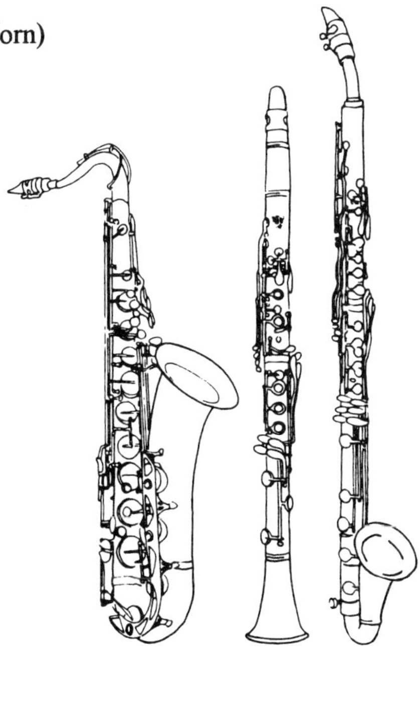

Music Is Forever

There was a young fellow who, among other subjects in school, had a class on the football field followed by band. During the games he warmed the bench and in a season, managed to get all of 7½ minutes on the field in the games. One day he was late for band practice, having been straining to be noticed by the coach to get a rare chance at a summer athletic camp program. When he finally went into the band room, his band teacher admonished, "You can turn out for football, baseball, basketball, and whatever, but after you finish school, that will probably be the end of participation sports. Just remember this:

Music is forever

The student didn't qualify for the summer sport's camp so he kissed the athletic department good-bye. Then he signed up for a summer National Drum Major camp at his own expense. That fall, he was back on the football field for every game, but instead of wearing a football outfit and warming the bench, he was the Drum Major and directed the band's half-time shows. That was a long time ago. Does he now participate in contact sports? Only on Monday nights with the TV, if there is time. Now in mid-life, he is still in music, as is his wife. And so are his kids.*

---

* Train up a child in the way he should go and when he is old be will not depart from it."
—Provb. 22:6

Music has always been a challenge for those who play well and want to make a career of it. This challenge is not a new phenomenon. The Big Band musicians earned a good pay. Some popular musicians do very well. But the Saturday Night dance musicians often can't get enough steady work to feed themselves let alone a family. The theme, "Don't give up the day job" is very realistic.

When the late Tony Lausmann was a mere tot, his ambition was to be a musician or an actor. Everyone in his family, who lived in the musical instrument craftsman's city of Grazlitz, Bohemia, was a player of something. This included his dad, who was a violinist, clarinetist and whatall, because he played them all before they left his bench. Dad was a precision musical instrument repairman. Dad often fixed an instrument to receive only promises of payment from the owners. Accordingly, Dad would not allow young Tony to learn to read music admonishing, "*Dir musikanten sind immer hungrig!*" —"Musicians are always hungry!" His dad paid an old gentleman to teach Tony how to play a concertina – totally useless in a formal band as there was no music written for concertinas.

Tony spent his career in the timber business. (In the Rogue River Valley, in 1940, he founded Kogap Manufacturing Company – dimension lumber, later plywood.) But music was always his first love. When labor negotiations with a union became heated, he'd reach under the table, haul out a concertina, and break the tense situation by playing music. Later he formed the Lausmann's Lousy Loggers Band in which Tony played his concertina. The other volunteer musicians, an aggregation of timber men with saxes, trumpets, trombone, string bass and drums, often faked it. Duke McQueen, of the present Shrine Band and Symphonic Band, was one of the drummers.

For Tony, to his dying day, as well as for uncounted others right down to the present time, "Music is forever."

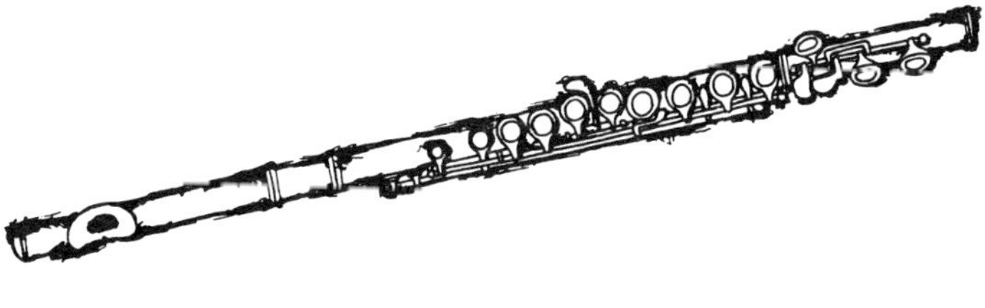

The *Hillah* Temple Shrine Band at Klamath Falls - 1959

BACK ROW: Henry Enders, Dr. Marcus Woods, _____ Woodley, Chas. Cook, Ray Schumacher, Ross Adams, Stew Norton, Bob Church, Dr. B. Cope, Dr. Chris Hald, Paul Workman, Neal Stone, Dick Cottle, Fred Strang, Mack Jones, Dave Fortmiller, Raoul Maddox, Phil Gates, Irv Mirick, Clarence Bell

FRONT ROW: Stan Morgan, Ray Anders, Bob Reinhold, Ned Marrs. Bill Laurine, Bill Abbott, Dr. Milo Kubalek, Harvey Woods, Ray Allred, Clyde Lees

The Southern Oregon Symphonic Band and Its Ancestors

The present Band is a direct descendant from its ancestor, the *Hillah* Temple Shrine Band. The Temple was authorized in 1909 and a part of the original charter states that the Temple was to have a Band.

Over the years, many dozens of men were a part of the Band. This was an award-winning, sharp-looking, quick-stepping uniformed marching Band complete with Glockenspiel and Drum Major. For quite a while, then young Dr. Chris Hald was the Drum Major. During one interval, this Band numbered over eighty members with its combined Drum and Bugle Corps.

There was a time, during the 1970's and 80's, when enthusiasm for belonging to fraternal orders declined. This was not unique to the Masonic Orders. It hit the Elks, Odd Fellows, Eagles, Knights of Pythias, Knights of Columbus, Order of Redmen – all of them. *Hillah* Shrine Temple was not exempt from this phenomenon. Its membership fell off through the demise of the old timers, and, during this period, fewer young men were

The Shrine Band was known far and wide as a fine Concert and Marching Band. Its membership was limited to members of the Shrine and its primary function was to play for Shrine-related events. The official name of the organization is Imperial Council of the Ancient Arabic Order of the Nobles of the Mystic Shrine of North America – also known as Shriners. Pictured is the Hillah Temple Shrine Band of Ashland, Oregon.

Ashland's Shrine Band with Drum Major Chris Hald, MD.

joining. The effect on the Shrine Band was in direct proportion to what was happening elsewhere – decline.

After a time, the band had shrunk so badly that there was no longer a balance of instrumentation so it was decided to change the name from "*Hillah* Temple Shrine Band," to the Southern Oregon Men's Band and invite non-Masons to join. W*ithin* this new organization was the Shrine Band, with its own Director. It would continue to exist and would perform for Shrine functions.

With the removal of the requirement for being a Mason, as a prerequisite for admittance into an expanded Band, membership in the new group enjoyed an immediate infusion of fresh adult* blood from the community. But even with this, there was still an imbalance to the instrumentation. As an example, the Band had lost all of its Flutes and Piccolos and many of its reeds. But there were quite a number of women flutists, as well as other band-type women musicians, throughout the community. Ah ha!

Would the Temple have difficulty if women joined this expanded Band? The "official" Shrine Band, although small, still played the official functions. It was decided there was no conflict with the Charter. Accordingly, the word seeped out that competent adult female musicians would be welcome.

* Because there are "spirits" – adult libations – in the Temple hall where most rehearsals are conducted, all Band members are a minimum of 21 years of age.

Ashland's Shrine Band with Drum Major Chris Hald, MD. Location, date unknown but autos are mid-1950 models.

Hillah Band Wins 2nd Place In Seattle

1963

The local Hillah Shrine Band took second place in a contest in Seattle during the Pacific Northwest Shrine Association Convention June 5 and 6.

The Saturday parade of bands was entered by approximately 20 bands from Oregon, Washington, Idaho, Montana, British Columbia, Alberta, and Wyoming. First place was awarded to Billings, Mont.

The Hillah band is primarily a concert band. The members are drawn from Ashland, Medford, and as far away as Roseburg. Irving Mirick of Medford is director.

More than 25 thousand Shriners attended the two-day convention.

—Ashland *Daily Tidings*

Ashland Shrine Band on parade at a Shrine convention in Reno, Nevada.

At this writing, 45 percent of the active membership of the Southern Oregon Symphonic Band are women.

The Southern Oregon Symphonic Band operates with an elected set of officers and a Board of Control. The musicians on the Board are appointed by and serve at the convenience of the President. Regular meetings are conducted during a light breakfast at a local restaurant.

One of the major responsibilities of the Board of Control is to hire a Director and agree on the Director's compensation as well as providing the Director with a job description. In short, the Director handles all musical decisions as to what compositions will be rehearsed and what pieces will be played on concerts. (The Southern Oregon Symphonic Band is not a marching Band although nearly 70 percent of its members have former marching experience.) The Director appoints a Concert Master usually at the beginning of the year. To augment other income, members donate a small annual fee. These funds apply toward the honorarium presented to the Director for his professional services. No records are kept as to who donates, as from time-to-time there are some members who love band music and are encouraged to play in the band but are unable to donate.

The band year is mid-September through early June. The Director works as a teacher in assisting the various sections of the band, as well as individuals, on the performance of the various compositions. The Southern Oregon Symphonic Band is a group of musicians concerned with:

Intonation

Tone Quality

Balance

Articulation

Dynamics

There is, occasionally, a certain "musical chairs" effect as the members, especially among the Clarinets and Trumpets, change seats to gain experience with the different parts. As a result, rehearsals, although always serious, can be quite lively.

The Band is sponsored by *Hillah* Shrine Temple and the rehearsals are generally held in the Temple.

By pronouncement of the Board of Control, all of the rehearsals and nearly all of the public performances are on Tuesday nights. This "standing order" provides stability to the band and encourages the members to discipline their time to keep Tuesday nights open just for the Band. While there are individual conflicts, members who are unable to attend rehearsals are encouraged to telephone the Director in advance. As happened on one occasion, the Director planned on rehearsing a novelty number that featured one section of the Band. Mercy! None of those players showed up therefore, the agenda for the rehearsal had to be changed at the last minute.

Rehearsals start promptly. On arrival, each member picks up the evening's program at the door, sets up, then adjusts music according to the printed agenda. Promptly, without announcement, the Director mounts the podium and neighborly chatter ceases. When the baton comes down, the rehearsal is under way.

A typical rehearsal contains music that is familiar, a detailed

Statistics of the Band
as Taken From the Questionnaires * (65 Participants)

Average age of the members: 60

35	(54%)	have college/university degrees
22	(34%)	have advanced college or university degrees
26	(40%)	had formal instrumental music training above high school
11	(15%)	have been hired to teach instrumental music in schools
26	(40%)	have military service in World War II
18	(28%)	charter members of Southern Oregon Symphonic Band
All	(100%)	live in Jackson County
19	(29%)	live in Ashland
24	(37%)	live in Medford
15	(23%)	are Shriners

Number of children of the Band members: 105 - l.6 children / member.

— * October 25, 1994

exercise and challenge in sight reading (something from the vast library), and careful rehearsal of music targeted for a public performance. As the level of competence varies widely in this volunteer community Band, there is always something for everyone.

The band's membership ranges from musicians who are self-taught through every level of experience to college Professors of Music. On the present roster, there are some who, years ago, barely finished high school to eleven school and college instrumental music teachers, some retired. All love to play music and have found that here is their opportunity to do it. One pointed out:

"Anyone can be a soloist. To be able to play with somebody else, as in a band, that's musicianship."

How to Join the Band

Adults of the extended community (approximately Jackson and Josephine Counties) who would like to play in the Southern Oregon Symphonic Band, might visit a rehearsal and afterward speak to the Director or, write to the Editor. Enclose a self-addressed stamped envelope for an application. The address is in the front of this book.

Instrumentation*

The order of seating in the Band is open except for the marked positions

DIRECTOR

John E. Drysdale

FLUTE

Jodi O'Connell – (Principal)
Sharon James
Kathleen Finnegan
Jeannette Marshall
Tionne Smith

OBOE

Glenn Matthews – (Principal)
Kathleen Mackris

BASSOON

Catharine Sleppy

CLARINET (B*b*)

Frank Brugman (Concert Master)
Pat Collins
George Stephen
Virginia Westerfield
Ron Bartlett
Margaret Wilson

ALTO CLARINET

Betty Brugman

BASS CLARINET

Larry Ware

ALTO SAXOPHONE

Sheldon James
Sylvia Schmeling

TENOR SAXOPHONE

Justin Dyrud – (Principal)
Charles Shuttle

* The instrumentation shown is subject to change as members leave and new people join.

BARITONE SAXOPHONE

Jean Powell

TRUMPET

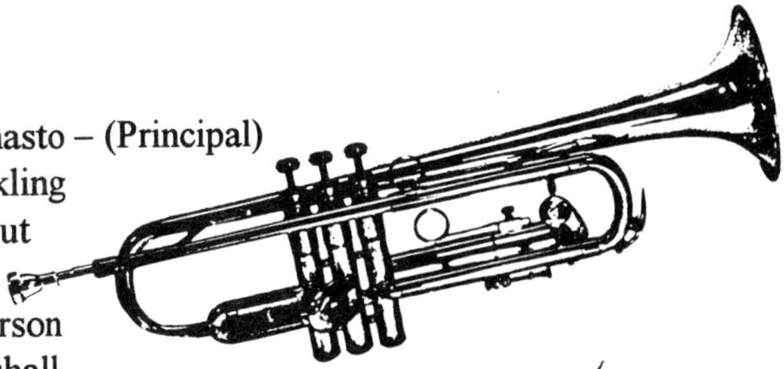

Harry Kannasto – (Principal)
Nelson Hickling
Beverly Spjut
Jim Kendle
Carol Anderson
Harry Marshall
Enrique Grunbaum
Kent Smith

FRENCH HORN

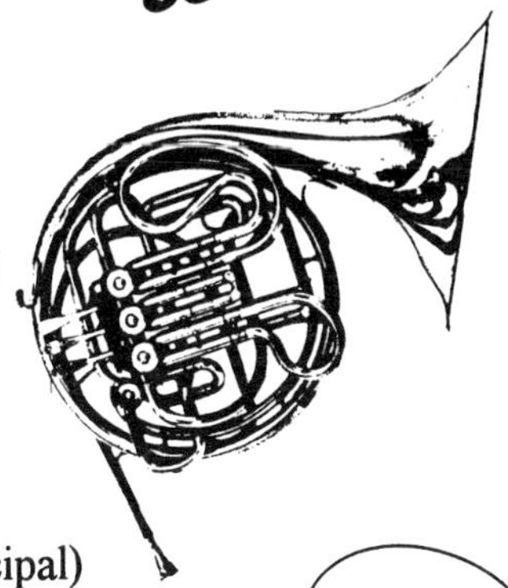

Mike Cady – (Principal)
Melissa Stowe
Shirley Donnelly
John Purcell

TROMBONE

Randy Hugdahl – (Principal)
John Stowe
Dick Finnell
Phil Gates
Larry Carlson
Charles Gabrenas
Gary Malone

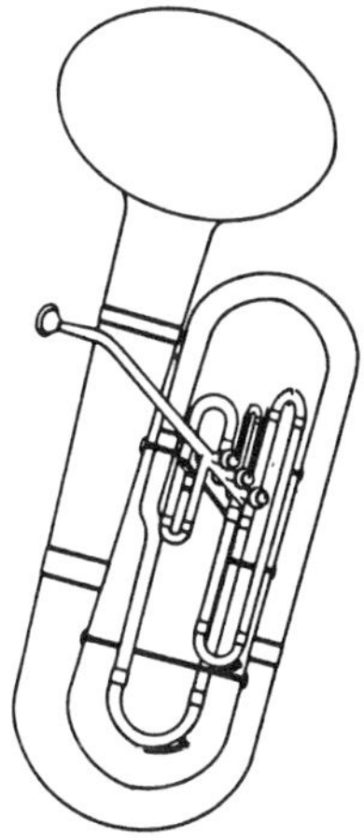

BARITONE HORN

Harvey Woods – (Principal)
Neil Stone
Bert Webber
Arne Jensen

BASS HORN

Preston Mitchell - BB*b* Tuba – (Principal)
Chris Hald - BB*b* Tuba
John Sleppy - F & BB*b* Tuba
Bill Schackelford - BB*b* Sousaphone
Robert Scholl - E*b* Tuba

PERCUSSION

Z. W. "Bill" Laurine - Bass Drum/Cymbals
Duke McQueen - Snare Drum
Hugh Littlebury - Snare Drum - Bells
Chuck George - Percussion

RECENT ALUMS

Members who have left the Band due to employment conflicts, health, retirement, moved away, etc.

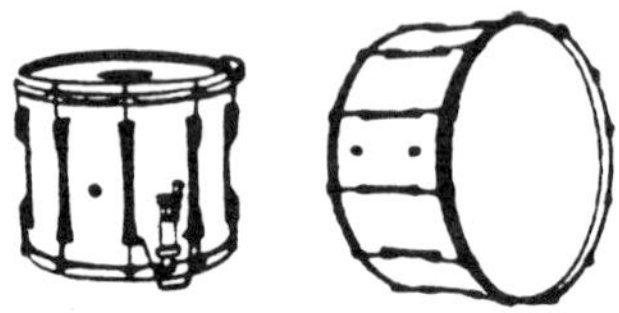

Julia Beattie, Flute
Bob Burdic, Alto Saxophone
Garrett Edmands, Snare Drum
Bob Hansen, Clarinet
Frank Hunnicutt, Clarinet
Don Hayden, Trumpet
Barbara Hunt, Bassoon
Hans Lindner, Oboe
Irv Mirick, Timpani
Maurice "Mickey" Morelli, French Horn
Cynthia Raymond, Flute
Leo Stan, Clarinet

Spin-off Aggregations

Hillah Temple Shrine German Band, Its Beginning and Its Growth Over the Years
Hillah Temple Shrine Desperation Seven
Hillah Saints Jazz Ensemble
Swing Kings Big Band
Hand Bell Festival Brass Sextet

The Hillah Temple Shrine German Band, Its Beginning and Its Growth Over the Years

By: Chris Hald

In 1961, it was recognized that there was a need in Hillah Temple of the Shrine to have a small musical group to provide entertainment for various Temple functions. This was proposed as a group of Shrine musicians of a considerably smaller number than made up the Hillah Temple Concert and Marching Band.

Coupled with this need, there was a desire of certain members of the Hillah Temple Shrine Band to form and be a part of such a smaller group. Accordingly, the Hillah Temple German Band was born.

Mr. Charles Cook, (Deceased) CWO (Ret) USA, former Army Band Director, was the director of the Shrine Band at that time. He agreed to rehearse the new German Band. The original members of this new group were Clyde W. Lees, (Deceased) Trumpet; Ray Aired, (Deceased) Trumpet; Phil Gates, Trombone; Chris Hald, M. D., Tuba; Duke McQueen, Snare Drum; Bill Laurine, Bass Drum. The Director, Mr. Cook, also played the Clarinet.

The first rehearsals were held in the back room of the carpet store (Laurine's Carpet House and Rug Barn) then owned by the

Hillah Temple Shrine Band and Men's Chorus (left, rear).

bass drummer and cymbal; crasher, Bill Laurine. (He has since retired.) This was on Riverside Avenue in Medford.

Finally the band had enough courage, though possibly not enough skill, to play in public, but decided to give it a try. The first public appearance was at a Shrine Band Summer Party held at the residence of Dr. Marcus Woods on High Street in Ashland. Since we were playing for "Our Own," we felt we could survive the musical criticism of the other members of the Shrine Band. To everyone's surprise, our efforts were well received.

The German Band played for various Temple functions for the next year. It was then decided that we should have the instrumentation of a typical Bavarian "Oompha Band." The first step was to obtain authentic music and German uniforms. Chris Hald had a former military friend, now a colonel, stationed in Munich, Germany. They had each played in the high school band in Minnesota decades earlier. A letter was written stating our needs. Soon we had a library of truly German arrangements of typical Bavarian music. The band uses the *Hungry Five German*

German Band, also known as the Bavarian Band.

Snapshot during a German band outing, (left to right) Clyde Lees, Duke McQueen, Chris Hald

Band Book. The harmonies developed in this aggregation were reminiscent of the typical old German Beer Gardens. We also purchased our original German Lederhosen.

The membership slowly grew until the instrumentation was three Clarinets, three Trumpets, Trombone. French Horn, Tuba, Bass Drum and two Snare Drums.

The players in those early years where all Shriners. The Trumpeters were Harry Kannasto, Clyde W. Lees, (Deceased) Dr. Harvey Woods, M.D. and Carol Anderson, R. Ph. The Clarinets were Willard Smith, Dr. Jerry Dyrud, Ed.D, and Mr. Charles Cook (Deceased). Phil Gates played Trombone. Clarence Bell (Deceased) former head of music at Montana State University, played Baritone Horn. Dr. Chris Hald played Sousaphone or Tuba depending on the occasion. Bill Laurine had the Bass Drum and Lowell Anderson, R. Ph. and S. V. "Duke" McQueen, former CEO of KOGAP Manufacturing Company, played Snare Drums.

At the time that the Hillah German Band was born, a similar band was created by the Douglas County Shrine Club in Roseburg, Oregon. The members of both bands know each other through Shrine. From time to time, The Ashland German Band would be short a player and the same would happen to the Roseburg German Band. Each band helped the other whenever it could be arranged. In the Roseburg Band, Harvey Kring, M. D. play Trombone as did ____Babbitt, M. D.; and a Dentist played Clarinet; Bob Keefe, a Lieutenant in the Oregon State Police, played Sousaphone. Clyde Carstens, (Deceased) founder and director of the Roseburg German Band, played Clarinet; Lowell Roden, in the funeral business, played Trumpet.

Both bands helped each other to survive for many years. Eventually, the Roseburg German Band broke up as some members moved away and others passed on.

In the 1960s and early 1970s, the Hillah Temple Shrine Band had a membership of 55. The German Band, as a part of the Shrine Band, played for the Imperial Sessions of the Shrine of North America in Vancouver, Canada; Seattle, Washington; Portland, Oregon; San Francisco, California; Reno, Nevada; Spokane, Washington and many other places in Northern California and Oregon.

Over the years, interest in Fraternal Orders diminished as did the membership of the Shrine Band. In time, the Hillah Temple Shrine Band decided to sponsor the Southern Oregon Men's Symphonic Band which was made up of both Shriners and non-Shriners. At a later date, the Shrine Band decided to change the name of the Southern Oregon Men's Symphonic Band to the Southern Oregon Symphonic Band and to invite adult women to be a part of the new expanded Symphonic Band. The German Band currently includes both men and women and is made up of both Shriners and Non-Shriners. Membership in the German Band is contingent on being a partricipating member in the parent Band, the Southern Oregon Symphonic Band.

The German Band now plays principally for entertainment of the Nobility of Hillah Temple at its monthly meetings and at various Octoberfests through out Southern Oregon and Northern

California. The membership now varies depending on the time those playing in the German Band have available to participate. This Band may be small in numbers, but its sound is rollicking, lusty and happy as its members "whoop it up" making great music and having fun.

At this writing the basic membership is:

Trumpet
Harry Kannasto (Director)
Carol Anderson
Nelson Hickling
Jim Kendle

Clarinet
Larry Ware
George Stephen
Ron Bartlett
Virginia Westerfield
Leo Stan
Willard Smith

French Horn
John Purcell
Mike Cady

Trombone
Phil Gates

Tuba
Chris Hald

Drums
Bill Laurine
Duke McQueen
Lowell Anderson
Hans Linder (drums and vocal)

Early Ensemble of the German Band (early 1960's)
(Left to right) Clarence Bell, Bob Burdic, Chris Hald, Charles Cook, Clude Carstens, Phil Gates, Clyde Lees

The Hillah Temple Shrine Desperation Seven

By: Chris Hald MD

One afternoon about 10 years ago (1984), a phone call was received by Chris Hald, MD., from the Hillah Temple office. The caller declared, "Doc, we need music desperately for the Temple meeting this Friday." I answered:

> You've got it ! The Desperation Seven will be there to play for you.

I got together some Dixieland music books. Then I made some phone calls to line up some musicians from the Southern Oregon Symphonic Band. Frank Brugman, retired Electrical Engineer, agreed to play Clarinet. Dr. Jerry Dyrud, Ed. D. in

Music, and former music teachers in many schools, agreed to play Tenor Sax. Harry Kannasto, Retired from the Music Department of the Medford, Oregon School District, said he would play Trumpet. Raoul Maddox, Director of Music for the Ashland, Oregon High School Music Department, agreed to play Trombone. Dave Wight, also a member of the Ashland High School Music Department, said he would come to play piano. Dr. Chris Hald MD., with his String Bass, and Lowell Anderson, R.Ph., agreed to play drums. The Desperation Seven was on its way.

Our first performance was for the social hour prior to the monthly Temple dinner and meeting. This first meeting of the Desperation Seven was a sight-reading rehearsal and performance combined. The Nobles attending the meeting did not seem to notice that this group had not rehearsed this music together before. They enthusiastically enjoyed themselves as we tooted out good old standard Dixieland tunes that they all recognized.

After that first performance, other Symphonic Band members have played with us. At times, Dave Wight would switch to Clarinet and Irv Mirick, former Director of Music for the Medford, Oregon School District, would fill in on the Piano. When Irv was not at the Piano, he would play Trap Drums in the absence of Lowell Anderson. Randy Hugdahl, a long time friend from World War W-II days, and former Army Bandsman, who worked for the U. S. Postal Service (now retired), took over the Trombone when Raoul Maddox was "snow birding" in the south.

The playing of music by the Desperation Seven has been largely for the pleasure of the members of Hillah Temple. But we have played a few times for the Ashland High School Class Reunions. So far all of this effort has been volunteer but we have had all kinds of fun and enjoyment from performing. That is what music is all about – fun in providing pleasure for both the players and the audience. The Desperation Seven fulfills these goals admirably. □

Jazz Ensemble: Glenn Matthews, Dewey ___, Carol Anderson, Harry Kannasto

Hillah Saints Jazz Ensemble

By: Harry Kannasto

This spin-off group was put together to play music extemporaneously with a dedication toward improvisation. It was felt that a large, varied repertoire for dancing must be well-learned as well as well-rehearsed. The group had to be highly versatile so it could perform in a small room or outdoors alongside a garden swimming pool.

The Hillah Saints plays Dixieland, popular ballads and Latin tunes all with ease. The compact sound this jazz band puts out is enjoyed at Shrine events as well as at public parties and dances.

The Hillah Saints Jazz Ensemble has these members at this writing:

Trumpet
Harry Kannasto (Director)
Carol Anderson

Tenor Saxophone
Glenn Matthews

Trombone
Dewey Meridyth

Piano
Don Bieghler
Foss Kramer (1974-84)

String Bass/Tuba
Chris Hald

Drums
Lowell Anderson

The Swing Kings Big Band plays for important conventions and formal dances. Although this Big Band is not a Shrine affiliated organization, its members are mainly from the Southern Oregon Symphonic Band which is sponsored by Hillah Temple Shrine.

Swing Kings Big Band

By: Harry Kannasto

When Harry Kannasto retired from teaching Instrumental Music in the Medford School District in 1986, one of his goals was to organize and direct a dance band that was capable of playing the Big Band sounds of the 1940's.

Since he was a member of Hillah Temple Shrine, which sponsored the Southern Oregon Men's Symphonic Band, this band was the logical place from which to seek members for the new Big Band. The immediate goal was reached when seventeen members indicated they'd like to fill a musical *niche*, by playing together and developing a Big Band sound.

Each year the Swing Kings play for many of the major social events throughout the Rogue River Valley. These include formal balls and convention dances.

At this writing, the band has these members:

Woodwinds
Frank Brugman
Frank Hunnicutt
Bill Jacoby
Jerry Dyrud
Tom Muller

Trumpets
Harry Kannasto (Director)
Nelson Hickling
Richard Cottle
Carol Anderson

Trombones
Randy Hugdahl
Dave Hoxie
John Stowe
Dick Finnell

Rhythm
Mickey Morelli (Piano)
Craig Mather (Drums)
Chris Hald (String Bass/Tuba)

Past Members: Warren Moore (T.Sax); George Stephens (A.Sax); Don Hayden (Trumpet); Raoul Maddox (Trombone); Eric Anderson (Piano); Rudy Domitrovich (Drums)

Hand Bell Festival Brass Sextet

By: Bert Webber

This brass ensemble was created over a decade ago to fill a unique place in the variety of Rogue Valley musical opportunities. Every spring, usually in early May, between 500 and 600 Hand Bell ringers assemble in Medford. They are in town to participate in the regional festival of the American Guild of English Hand Bell Ringers.

The majority of the bell choirs are sponsored by a wide variety of churches and schools. The trip for a week-end to the festival in Medford, is looked upon as the annual highlight trip of many of these choirs. They come mostly from Oregon, California, Washington, Nevada.

To enhance the formal concert on Saturday night, a group of musicians from the Southern Oregon Symphonic Band formed the Hand Bell Festival Brass Sextet to provide accompaniment. In addition to setting a foundation for the Bells for the Grand Opening of the concert with the playing of the "Star Spangled Banner," the Brass Sextet accompanies the hundreds of ringers for a major Hand Bell concert composition.

At this writing the personnel of the Sextet are:

Harry Kannasto, (Trumpet – Director)
Nelson Hickling, Trumpet
Melissa Stowe, French Horn
Randy Hugdahl, Trombone
John Stowe, Trombone
Preston Mitchell, BB*b*-Tuba

Southern Oregon Symphonic Band
Lithia Park – Ashland, Oregon
7 PM –June 7, 1994

—Program—

The Star Spangled Banner	Francis Scott Key
My Heart Stood Still	Richard Rodgers
The Klaxon (March)	Henry Fillmore
You'll Never Walk Alone	Richard Rodgers
Chaconne, (from First Military Suite)	Gustav Holst
Theme From the Movie *superman*	John Williams
Zampa (Overture)	L.J.F. Herold
His Honor (March)	Henry Fillmore
I Left My Heart in San Francisco	George Cory
Hollywood Jubilee	Nacio Herb Brown
Should I, Pagan Love Song, Doll Dance, Temptation	
Americans We (March)	Henry Fillmore
Armed Forces Salute	Arr. Bob Lowden
Caisson Song, Semper Paratus, Marine's Hymn, Air Force, Anchors Away	
Washington Post (March)	John Philip Sousa

The Southern Oregon Symphonic band is sponsored by the Ashland Hillah Temple. Financial support is obtained through contributions from the Hillah Temple Shriner's German Band, and by donations made by groups for which we perform. We all thank our Band President, Dr. Christian P. Hald (ret), for working with the Ashland Parks and recreation Commission to make this concert possible. As director, I would like to acknowledge Harry Kannasto and Carol Anderson for coordinating the physical setup of the band at our concerts. I also wish to express my appreciation to each member of the Band for sharing their talents. —John E. Drysdale, Director

" Ralph Leach, a long time "Union" Trumpet man, who swims with me at the YMCA, said our [Southern Oregon Symphonic Band] was the best band he had ever heard in the Ashland City Park!!" —G. Ross Adams

A corner of the German Band. (left to right) Anton "Tony" Lausmann with Concertina; Herb Grueling, Clarinet; Ross Adams, Sousaphone; Warren Moore, Clarinet.

Biographical Sketches

DECEASED

G. Ross ADAMS (BB*b* Sousaphone)
Born: (McDonald, Pa.) Dec. 1, 1912 – Aug. 28, 1994
Married

EDUCATION
Aliquippa, High School, Aliquippa, Pa.
West Virginia University (Two terms)

BEGAN STUDYING INSTRUMENTAL MUSIC
Tuba - 7th Grade.

PRINCIPAL INSTRUMENTAL TEACHERS
D. A. Davenport. " He played with John Philip Sousa Band on a two year tour. Davenport composed many marches and songs – taught Henry Mancini the Flute."

MUSICAL GROUPS
Ashland City Band - 43 years
Hillah Temple Shrine Band, 1950 –
Hillah Temple German Band
Southern Oregon Symphonic Band, Charter Member
" Ralph Leach, a long time "Union" Trumpet man, who swims with me at the YMCA, said our [Southern Oregon Symphonic Band] was the best band he had ever heard in the Ashland City Park!!"

Three children, – grown

Carol D. ANDERSON (Trumpet)

Born: (Stanley, N.Dakota) Oct. 31, 1927
Married: "Marge" (1958)

EDUCATION
Stanley High School Grad. 1945
University of North Dakota, York, N.D.
North Dakota State College, Fargo, N.D., BS Pharmacy/Chemistry. 1949

BEGAN STUDYING INSTRUMENTAL MUSIC
With friends in *Hillah* Temple Shrine Band – 1963

MUSICAL GROUPS
Various small groups including: Anderson's "Halloween Band"
Hillah Temple Shrine Band - 30 years
Hillah Temple Swing Kings
Southern Oregon Symphonic Band - Charter Member

MILITARY SERVICE
Regular Army - First Occupation of Japan (Yokohama, Kobe) after World War II Service in Guam, Philippines, Okinawa.

OCCUPATION - PROFESSION
Pharmacologist - Druggist (Retired)
Served 10 years on School Board, Ashland, Ore.

HONORS AND AWARDS
Welterweight Boxing Championship (college) TKE Fraternity

AT HOME: Ashland, Ore. Two children – grown

Ronald W. "Ron" BARTLETT (B*b*-Clarinet)

Born: (Salem, Ore.) Dec. 30, 1928
Married: Gloria (1965)

EDUCATION
Salem High School, Grad. 1948
Willamette University, BM. 1954
Willamette Univ. M.Ed. 1957
Graduate work at Boston Univ.

BEGAN STUDYING INSTRUMENTAL MUSIC
Clarinet, age 8,
Salem Youth City Band
Master Bread Bakery Band

PRINCIPAL INSTRUMENTAL TEACHERS: Vernon Wiscarson
Elementary and High school - Salem.
Jr. High School - Carl Thielen

PRIVATE TEACHERS
Vernon Wiscarson - Clarinet
Don Jessup, Willamette Univ. - Clarinet
Mabel Teal - Piano
Albert Perfect - Clarinet

MUSICAL GROUPS
Salem school bands; Salem City Band
Willamette Univ. Band and Orchestra
Ashland City Band
560th U.S. Air Force Band, 1950-52
Southern Oregon Symphonic Band 1993–
Directed:
Handel's Messiah" in Medford, Ore - 21 years
Hedrick Jr. High School Band - 33 years
Choir, First Christian Church, Medford - many years

MILITARY SERVICE
U. S. Air Force - Korean War 1950-52
560th USAF Band, Spokane, Moses Lake, Tacoma, Wash.
Presented weekly show, "March On" over KING-TV in Seattle, Wash.

OCCUPATION - PROFESSION
Band Director - Madras, Oregon 19554-56
Band Director - Hedrick Jr. High School, Medford, Ore. 33 years

AT HOME: Medford, Ore. Two children – grown

John Drysdale directs the Symphonic Band during the Lithia Park Concert on June 7, 1994.

Betty BRUGMAN (Alto Clarinet)

Born: (Minnesota) June 17, 1925

Married: Frank Brugman. (1948)

EDUCATION

Elementary schools – 1-room country Dist. 12; 32, Old Glory, Minn.
Goodridge High School, Goodridge, Minn.
Scappoose High School, Scappoose, Ore. Grad. 1942.
Oregon State College. BA Science and Liberal Arts 1947.

BEGAN STUDYING INSTRUMENTAL MUSIC

Goodridge, Minn. Clarinet in school band 1939

PRINCIPAL INSTRUMENTAL TEACHERS

Vern Hagen, school band, Goodridge, Minn.
Delbert Moore, OSC orchestra and band

PRIVATE TEACHERS

Craig Woods, Trombone, Ventura, Calif.

MUSICAL GROUPS

Three Community College bands in Southern California
Southern Oregon Symphonic Band, 1992

OCCUPATION - PROFESSION

Homemaker

"I heard the Sousa Band directed by John Phillip himself at the Minnesota State Fair. Unfortunately, I was only two years old and don't remember a note, but my mother said that I enjoyed the concert."

HONORS AND AWARDS

EUTERPE – Music Honorary, Oregon State College

AT HOME: Talent, Ore. Three children – grown

Frank Brugman, Concert Master
with Virginia Westerfield seated behind

Frank BRUGMAN (B♭-Clarinet) (Concert Master)

Born: (Oak Park, Ill.) Feb. 5, 1923

Married: Betty Rae Johnson (1948)

EDUCATION

Hinsdale Township High School. Hinsdale, Ill. Grad. 1941

Northwestern Univ. BS CHE (Chemical Engineering) 1945

BEGAN STUDYING INSTRUMENTAL MUSIC

James L. Buckborough, Hinsdale High School

Captain Beard, Oregon State College Band 1941-42

Glen Cliff Bainum, Northwestern University. 1942

PRIVATE TEACHERS
Jerry Stowell (Chicago Symphony Orchestra) 1939-42

MUSICAL GROUPS
Hinsdale High School Band and Orchestra
Oregon State College Band, 1941-42
Northwestern University Band, 1942
Symphony Woods Orchestra, Western Springs, Ill., 1939-41
Columbia Univ. Midshipman School Band, 1945
Monterey Park Band, (Calif.), 1970-78
Ventura County (Calif.) Band, 1978-85
California Concert Band, 1982-85
Ventura County Symphony, 1984
Ashland City Band, 1985 –
Rogue Valley Wind Ensemble, 1988 –
Southern Oregon State College Band, 1985 –
Rogue Valley Symphony, 1985 –
Hillah Temple Shrine band, 1985 –
Southern Oregon Symphonic Band, Charter Member

MILITARY SERVICE
U. S. Navy 1943-46 (Lt.jg.) *USS Princeton* 1945-46

OCCUPATION - PROFESSION
U. S. Oil Refining Co. (President - Retired)
Oxnard Refinery (President – Retired)

AT HOME Talent, Ore. Three children – grown

→ALUM OF THE BAND – RETIRED

Robert L. "Bob" BURDIC DMD (Alto Saxophone)
Born: (Ashland, Ore.) Mar. 28, 1920
Married:

EDUCATION
Ashland High School, Ashland, Ore.
Southern Oregon Normal School, Ashland, Ore.
Southern Oregon College of Education, Ashland, Ore.
California School of Fine Arts
Art Center School of Design (Los Angeles, Calif.)
Univ. of Oregon Dental School. D.M.D. 1955

BEGAN STUDYING INSTRUMENTAL MUSIC
Piano ages 9-12.
Bass Drum, High School
"I picked up other instruments on my own - Clarinet, Tenor and Alto Saxophone, Baritone Horn."

PRIVATE TEACHERS
Hilma Enanden - Piano 1929-32

MUSICAL GROUPS
Band and Orchestra in High School - Bass Drum
Ashland City Band, Ashland, Ore. Saxophone and Baritone Horn, 1956-65
Hillah Temple Shrine Band
Southern Oregon Symphonic Band –1993 RETIRED

MILITARY SERVICE
5 years – World War II, Anti-Aircraft Artillery

OCCUPATION - PROFESSION
Photography
Dentistry

AT HOME: Ashland, Ore.

Michael CADY (French Horn)
Born: (Ashland, Ore.) Aug. 3, 1958
Married: Susan McNeil (1991)

EDUCATION
Ashland Senior High School. 1976
Oregon State University. BS Horticulture 1985

BEGAN STUDYING INSTRUMENTAL MUSIC
Walker Elementary School, Ashland, 5th Grade (Cornet) - Warren Moore 1968-70
French Horn, Junior High - Rudy Domitrovich 1970-73
High School - Raoul Maddox 1973-75
Oregon State Univ., Frank Kinney 1980-81; James Douglas, 1981-83

PRINCIPAL INSTRUMENTAL TEACHERS
Warren Moore 1968-70
Rudy Domitrovich 1970-73
Frank Kinney 1980-81
James Douglas 1981-83
Raoul Maddox, 1986

MUSICAL GROUPS
Oregon State Univ. Concert Band, 1980-83
Silver Cornet Band, 1988-90
Ashland City Band, 1979-80, 1986 –
Southern Oregon Symphonic Band - Charter Member
Hillah Temple German Band, 1989 –

OCCUPATION- PROFESSION
Horticulturist

AT HOME: Medford, Ore. One child (age 2)

Larry CARLSON (Trombone)
Born: (Madison, Wisc.) Feb. 19, 1949
Married: Bea

EDUCATION
Wilson High School, Long Beach, Calif. Grad. 1966
Long Beach State College, 1966-68
Univ. of California L.A., BA, Math 1970
Humboldt State Univ., Arcata, Calif. Teaching Cert.

BEGAN STUDYING INSTRUMENTAL MUSIC
Elementary School, 5th Grade, Long Beach, Calif.

PRINCIPAL INSTRUMENTAL TEACHERS
Rolland Sandberg, Wilson High School, 1963-66

MUSICAL GROUPS
Wally Martin's Associates 1982-92
Brass Choir 1992–
Southern Oregon Symphonic Band 1993 –

MILITARY SERVICE
U. S. Navy - 1971-73 (Personnel Clerk)

OCCUPATION - PROFESSION
Math Teacher - North Valley High School, Grants Pass, Ore.

AT HOME: Ashland. One child – grown

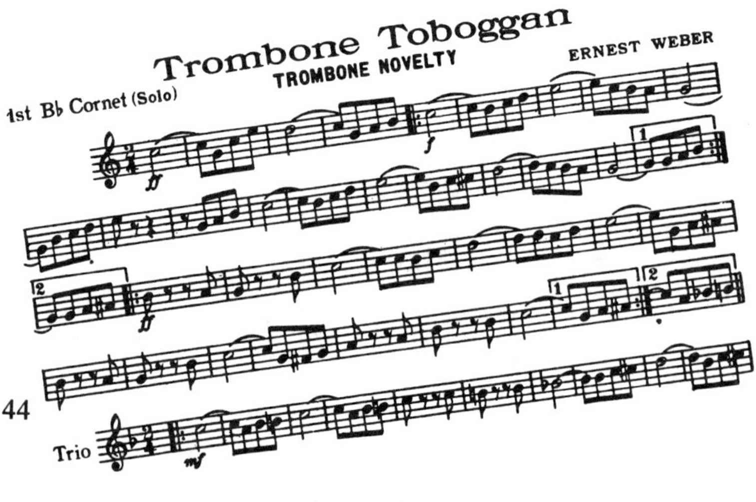

Versatile Pat Collins. Here with an Oboe, at right in her school days with an Alto Sax. In the present band she plays B*b*-Clarinet.

Pat COLLINS (B*b*-Clarinet)

Born: (Fresno, Calif.) Apr. 13, 1935
Married: Dana H. Riehl (1956)

EDUCATION

Coalinga, Calif. High School. Grad. 1953
Univ. of Oregon. BS Music Educ. 1956

BEGAN STUDYING INSTRUMENTAL MUSIC

School bands and orchestras:
4th grade - Clarinet
7th Grade - Clarinet and Violin
8th grade - Clarinet, Oboe
10th grade - Clarinet, Oboe, Saxophone

PRINCIPAL INSTRUMENTAL TEACHERS

"My father, J. Oscar Riehl, was my band/orchestra director grades 7-12."
Numerous summer sessions college bands and orchestras, 7th grade – on.
Univ. of Idaho, Univ. of Colorado, Univ. of Washington, Univ. of Oregon. Directors Sawhill, Revelli, Robertson (Oberlin), Bachman, etc.

PRIVATE TEACHERS
Russ Howland - Fresno State Univ.
Leland Lincoln, Oakland, San Antonio, Boston Pops Symphonies
Robert Vagner and Robert Cunningham, Univ. of Oregon

MUSICAL GROUPS
University of Oregon Band, Robert Dagner
Eugene Symphony, Edmund Cykler and George Boughton
Rogue Valley Symphony, Fred Palmer, etc. – 22 years
Ashland City Band, Raoul Maddox
Rogue Valley Wind Ensemble, Bill Norfleet
Siskiyou Chamber Orchestra
Rogue Valley English Handbell Festival (Oboe soloist)
Rogue Valley Opera
Southern Oregon Symphony Band 1992–
Numerous small ensembles, pit orchestras, opera orchestras.
Messiah, 22 years.

OCCUPATION - PROFESSION
School music teacher – substituted, all Rogue Valley Schools, 20 years
Private music teacher since 1951

HONORS AND AWARDS
Mu Phi Epsilon Music Honorary

AT HOME: Medford, Ore. Two children – grown

Shirley DONNELLY (French Horn)
Born: (Canyonville, Ore.) Mar. 4, 1953
Married: David Donnelly, MD (Pearl Harbor Day), 1974

EDUCATION
Riddle High School, Riddle, Ore. Grad. 1971
Oregon State Univ. (Undergrad)
Eastern Oregon State College (Undergrad)
Univ. of Oregon Medical School BS. Medical Technology.

BEGAN STUDYING INSTRUMENTAL MUSIC
Riddle High School - French Horn

PRINCIPAL INSTRUMENTAL TEACHERS
Butch Briery - Riddle High School
M. Max McKee - Southern Oregon State College
Raoul Maddox, Ashland City Band

Glenn Mathews (left) with Oboe and Shirley Donnelly, French Horn

MUSICAL GROUPS
American Band College Symphonic Band, 1985
Ashland City Band
Rogue Valley Symphony Orchestra
Southern Oregon State College Alumni Band
Rogue Valley Wind Ensemble
Rogue Valley Horn Club
Southern Oregon Symphonic Band, 1991 –

OCCUPATION- PROFESSION
Medical Technologist - Medford Clinic, Medford, Oregon.

AT HOME: Medford, Ore. Two children, 4, 11.

John Drysdale, Director, Southern Oregon Symphonic Band. (Lower) The Concert at V.A., Domiciliary Sept. 24, 1994.

John E. Drysdale as High School student. His feature instruments are Violin and French Horn.

John E. DRYSDALE (Director)
Born: (Lodi, Calif.) 1925.
Married: Betty Lou Walder Drysdale (1948)

EDUCATION
Sunnyside High School - Sunnyside, Wash. Grad. 1943
Univ. of Oregon BS. Music Education. 1950
Univ. of Oregon MM. (Master of Music) 1965
Southern Oregon State College Supervisor Cert. 1978

PRINCIPAL INSTRUMENTS
Violin - French Horn

PRINCIPAL BAND/ORCHESTRA TEACHERS
Karl Diettrich, Sunnyside, High School 1939-41
William Herbst, Sunnyside High School 1941-43
Rex Underwood, Univ. of Oregon 1946-47

John H. Drysdale, Violinist

Ed Cykler, Univ. of Oregon 1947-50
John Stehn, Univ. of Oregon 1946-50
Bob Vagner, Univ. Of Oregon 1963-65 (Summers)

PRIVATE TEACHERS

National Institute of Musical Arts, Sunnyside, Wash 1933-36. (Mr. Davis)
Geraldine Hinkston Colby, Sunnyside, Wash (Violin) 1936-42
Alfred Boyington, Washington State College, (Violin) Summer 1942
George Boughton, Univ. of Oregon, (Violin) 1946-50
Larry Maves, Univ. of Oregon (Violin) Summers 1963-65
Robert Hladkey, Univ. Oregon (Cello) Summer 1964

MUSICAL GROUPS

Sunnyside High School Band and Orchestra 1939-43
Yakima Symphony, Yakima, Wash. 1942-43
U. S. Navy - Station Band. Farragut, Idaho Summer 1943
Univ of Oregon Band and Orchestra 1946 -50 (includes summer sessions)
Medford Philharmonic (Viola - Ass't Cond.) [Richard Werner, Dir.] 1954-58
Southern Oregon Little Symphony (Viola) [Herbert Cecil, Dir.]
Univ. of Oregon Symphony, Concert Master (summers) 1963-65

MILITARY SERVICE

U. S. Navy sonar/radar operator aboard DE *Garfield Thomas.* Service in European, Pacific and Mediterranean Theaters of Operations 1943-46

OCCUPATION - PROFESSION

Musician - Teacher - Director

SCHOOL POSITIONS

Yoncalla Grade School, Yoncalla, Ore. 1949-50 Band Dir.
Klamath falls High School, Klamath Falls, Ore. 1950-52, Orchestra
Oregon Technical Institute, Klamath Falls, Ore. 1951-52 Band Dir.
Redmond High School, Redmond, Ore. 1952-53, Band Dir.
Medford High School, 1953-83.
Orchestra 1953-77; Inst. Supv. 1974-76; Mus. Ed. Supv. 1976-83; Ass't to Superintendent 1982-83

COMMUNITY CONDUCTING POSITIONS

Univ. of Oregon High School Summer Music Sessions Instr. 1955-1964
Rogue Valley Symphony, Concert Master / Guest Cond. 1963-74
Episcopal Church Choir Dir.- Medford 1955-65
Southern Oregon Symphonic Band. Dir. 1990 –

HONORS, AWARDS, SPECIAL OFFICES, POSITIONS HELD

Outstanding Musician Award. Wash. State College Music Camp, 1942
Phi Mu Alpha Honorary Music Fraternity, Univ. of Oregon., 1947
Orchestra Affairs Chairman, Oregon Music Educator's Assoc., elected twice
First Chair of American Award, 1976
Secretary-Treasurer, *Phi Delta Kappa*, 1978
Listed in *Who's Who in School District Officials* 1976
Selected for "Wall of Fame" Sunnyside High School, 1992
Medford Orchestra selected to perform at Northwest Music Educator's Conf. Seattle, 1977. (Received Certificate of Excellence)
Medford Orchestra selected to perform at EXPO-74 Spokane, Victoria BC.
Willamette Univ., Univ. of Oregon, Portland State Univ. 1955
Oregon Education Convention, Portland, 1956
Univ. of Oregon Music Conference, 1963
Portland State Univ. Music Conference, 1968
Victoria, B.C. Music Conference, 1971
Rotunda, State Capitol, 1973; Special Music Reviewer, Medford *Mail Tribune* 1963-65; Honored by Northwest Bandmasters Association in 1978. Military Decorations: Service Medals: European-African-Middle Eastern Theater; Asiatic-Pacific Theater; American Theater; Victory Medal.

AT HOME Medford, Ore. 2 children – grown

John E. Drysdale in 1994

Justin "Jerry" DYRUD Ed.D. (Tenor Saxophone)

Born: (Maddock, N.Dak.) April 19, 1919.

Married: Jeannette Ummel 1944

EDUCATION

Maddock N.Dak. High School, Grad. 1937

Concordia College, Moorhead, Minn. BA Political Science and Economics 1941

Univ of North Dakota, Grand Forks, N.D. MA Political Science and Education 1948

Concordia Conservatory, Fargo, N.D. BM. Vocal and Instr. Music 1947

Lewis and Clark College, Portland, Ore. Graduate Study: Arranging and Composition

Arizona State Univ. Music Conducting, 1952

Univ. of Oregon. Ed. D. 1959

Dissertation: *Qualification and Education of Elementary Teachers in Oregon*

BEGAN STUDYING INSTRUMENTAL MUSIC

Maddock High School - Woodwinds. 1935

Concordia College. - Saxophone. 1937-1941

Arizona state Univ. - Clarinet. 1952

Univ. of Oregon. - Brass instruments, 1957; String Bass. 1958

PRINCIPAL INSTRUMENTAL AND PRIVATE TEACHERS

Fred Klein, Woodwinds 1935

Sir John Holvik, Saxophone 1937-1941

John Stehn, Brass 1957

George Broughton, String Bass 1958

Ira Lee,

Kathryn Dean, Engebret Thormodsgaard, Max Miller, Exine Bailey - voice; Paul Christianson, voice and conducting and arranging.

MUSICAL GROUPS

Maddock High School Band 1934-37

Maddock-Benson County Band - 1935-37

Concordia College Band 1937-41

Univ. of N.Dakota Band 1947-48

Univ. of Oregon Band (Dir.) 1967-58

Arizona State Univ. Band 1952

Hillah Temple Shrine Band 35 years

Ashland City Band, Ashland, Ore. 5 years

Jack Goodall's Band

Jimmy Osgood Band

Swing Kings Band

Resurrection Seven Band

Tom Scott Band

Hillah Temple German Band – 35 years

Southern Oregon Symphonic Band, Charter Member

SCHOOL POSITIONS

Ulen, Minn. High School Band - 1941

Hillsboro High School Band, N.Dak., 1948

(Won First Place State Band Contest of 37 bands)

Barnesville High School Band, Minn.

(Chosen to play for Regional Basketball Tour 1947)

Silverton High School Band, Silverton, Ore. 1949-56

Vocal Music Supervisor and Elementary School Consultant, Medford School Dist., Medford, Ore. 1957-66

COMMUNITY CONDUCTING POSITIONS

Maddock Church Choir

Silverton High School Choir, Silverton, Ore.

Emanuel Lutheran Church Choir

Ascension Lutheran Church Choir - Medford, Ore.

Methodist Church Choir - Medford, Ore.

Westminster Presbyterian Church Choir Medford, Ore.

Medford Choralaires (adult chorus) Medford, Ore. 1957-58

Mt. Angel Male Chorus

OCCUPATION - PROFESSIONS

Mostly music - Now retired

"During my many years in Education, I have taught band and choir in North Dakota, Minnesota and Oregon and have been Principal and Ass't Supt. as well as Supervisor of Music. During the last ten years of my working life, I was editorial Consultant for the Publishing Division of Columbia Broadcasting System, and traveled extensively giving workshops and writing and revising texts for Music, Math, English and Social Studies. In this capacity I was Elementary Music Consultant for the Music Educators National Conference in Hawaii and El Paso and the Canadian National Music Educ. Conference in Calgary."

MILITARY SERVICE

Captain (Pilot), Wing Leader B-25 Group, 340th Medium Bomb Group, North Africa, Sicily, Italy, elsewhere in Europe.

Director of Air Force Ground School, Greenville S.C.

Director, Regional Program– Re-orientation and re-education of German POW's. Very controversial and possibly illegal under International Pacts.

Military Intelligence, Korean War and Intelligence Reserve

HONORS AND AWARDS

Distinguished Flying Cross; Air Medal w/7 Oak Leaf Clusters; Presidential Unit Citation w/2 Oak Leaf Clusters; British Eighth Army Commendation; European-African-Middle Eastern Theater Medal; North Africa campaign Medal; American Theater Medal; Victory Medal

AT HOME: Phoenix, Ore. Five children grown

→LEAVE OF ABSENCE

Garrett Petterson EDMANDS (Percussion)

Born: (Boston, Mass.) Oct. 19, 1951

Divorced

EDUCATION

Belmont Hill Prep School for Boys, Belmont, Mass. Grad. 1970

Beloit College, Beloit, Wisc. BA. Spanish 1974

BEGAN STUDYING INSTRUMENTAL MUSIC

"I began with the piano about 7 years old. When we moved, I went to popular piano and learned old-time style with a rhythm bass. Studied drums with a rudimentary teacher at age 12. I drove my parents crazy banging on tables so they bought me bongos."

PRINCIPAL INSTRUMENTAL TEACHERS

Staff teachers, Belmont Hill School

Mr. Donohue

Richard Bennett

PRIVATE TEACHERS

J. Wm. Pierce, Vancouver, Wash., Accordion

Gary Spellissey, Chelmsford, Mass., Percussion

MUSICAL GROUPS

Ashland City Band, Ashland, Ore. 1990 –

Southern Oregon Symphonic Band, 1992 –

OCCUPATION - PROFESSION

Construction Trade: Painter. Contractor

AT HOME: Ashland, Ore. One child.

Kathleen FINNEGAN (Flute)

Born: (Chicago, Ill.) Oct. 1, 1946

EDUCATION

Nazareth Academy (High School), Grad. 1964
Diablo Valley College (Pleasant Hill, Calif.) AA Liberal Arts, 1976
Southern Oregon State College (Ashland, Ore.)BS Psychology, 1978
John F. Kennedy Univ. (Orinda, Calif.) MA Counseling Psych - Transpersonal Specialization

BEGAN STUDYING INSTRUMENTAL MUSIC

Downers Grove, Ill. - 6th grade - flute 1956; piano 1952; voice - chorale/madrigal. Private study in classical and show.
High School Orchestra, LaGrange, Ill 1960-64
Nazareth Academy

PRIVATE TEACHERS

Debra Guy - Ashland, Ore. (classical flute) 1994
Ann Bass (voice) 1993-94

MUSICAL GROUPS

State of Jefferson Marching Band (flute)
Chamber Music groups in Southern Ore. and San Francisco
Southern Oregon Symphonic Band

MILITARY SERVICE

U.S. Navy Hospital Corps Emergency Room and X-ray Tech. Camp LeJuene, N.C. 1967-1970

OCCUPATION - PROFESSION

Therapist and Consultant Adults/Children - teacher and counselor

HONORS AND AWARDS

Magnum Cum Laude - Southern Oregon State College, 1978
Honor Guard, U.S. Navy (Bainbridge, Md.)

AT HOME: Ashland, Ore. Two children – grown

Richard H. "Dick" FINNELL (Trombone)

Born: (Pendleton, Ore.) Aug. 14, 1924
Married: Norma, 1950

EDUCATION

Washington School, Ashland, Ore.
Ashland Jr. High School
Ashland High School. Grad. 1942.
University of Oregon (Music Major) 1 year
Southern Oregon College 1947

Dick Finnell

BEGAN STUDYING INSTRUMENTAL MUSIC
Ashland Jr. High School - Sousaphone, 1939
Ashland High School - Trombone, 1941-42

PRINCIPAL INSTRUMENTAL TEACHERS
Gordon Tripp, High School 1940-42
John Stehn, Univ. of Oregon 1942-43
Rex Underwood, Univ. of Oregon 1942-43
Herbert Cecil, Southern Oregon State College, 1947-48

PRIVATE TEACHERS
Clarence Bubb (San Francisco Symphony - Trumpet) at Univ. of Oregon.
Jaroslav Cimera, Chicago, Ill. 1944-45 (He played Trombone with John Philip Sousa)

MUSICAL GROUPS
Univ. of Oregon Band, 1942-43
Univ. of Oregon Symphony Orchestra, 1942-43
346th Army Service Forces Band, 1943-46, Chicago Ill.
Various dance bands in Chicago including Eddie Howard, 1946-47.
Dick Finnell Dance Band, Ashland, Ore. 1941-42
Southern Oregon College Symphony
Ashland City Band, 1941-42, 1960-?, 1970-?
Hillah Temple Shrine Band, 1960 –
Southern Oregon Symphonic Band, Charter Member

MILITARY SERVICE
U. S. Army, April 1943 - March 1946
Fort Custer, Michigan M.P.R.T.C. Band
346th Army Service Forces Band, Chicago, Ill. (Vaughn General Hospital)

OCCUPATION - PROFESSION
Oregon State Police - Trooper 18 years 1948-1966
Jackson County Public Works & Planning Dept. 1967-1987 (Retired)

AT HOME: Phoenix, Ore. Two children – grown

Charles GABRENAS (Bass Trombone)
Born: (Chicago, Ill.) March 13, 1913
Married: Juanita 1942
EDUCATION: Tilden High School (Vocational courses), Chicago, Ill. Grad. 1928.

BEGAN STUDYING INSTRUMENTAL MUSIC
Tilden High School - Trombone - Chicago 1928

PRINCIPAL INSTRUMENTAL TEACHERS
Howard Stube - Chicago, 1928-32
George Goranson - Chicago, 1928-32

PRIVATE TEACHERS
Jerislav Cimera, 1933 - Oak Park, Ill.
Arnold Jacobs (Tuba, Chicago Symphony) 1950-52

MUSICAL GROUPS
Univ. of Chicago Band - 1933-34 (Trombone)
Chicago Black Horse Troop Band (30 piece - mounted) Trombone 1936-40
Davenport, Iowa 1940-50, Tri-City Symphony, Tenor Trombone, 1940-45 Bass Trombone, 1950-55
U. S. Naval Ordnance Plant Dance Band - Forest Park, Ill. 1945-48 (Trombone - Tuba)
Aldigen Town Band - Germany - 1971-74, (Trombone)
Al Bahr Shrine Band - San Diego, Calif. (Tuba, Baritone, Trombone) 1977-93
Palomar College Band. San Marcos, Calif. (Bass Trombone) 1977-84
Pomerado Town Band - Poway, Calif. (Tuba, Trombone) 1990-93
Southern Oregon Symphonic Band - 1993–

MILITARY SERVICE: U.S. Army Reserve, 106th Cavalry, 1936-40

OCCUPATION - PROFESSION
(Retired) Toolmaker, 15 years
Equipment Specialist, Army Weapons, 1950-77

AT HOME: Talent, Ore.

Army Bandsman Gabrenas played Trombone while on a horse

Philip GATES (Trombone)

Born: (Medford, Ore.) Oct. 2, 1926

Married: Shirley

EDUCATION

Roosevelt Elementary School - Medford, Ore.
McLoughlin Jr. High School - Medford, Ore.
Medford Sr. High School - Medford, Ore. Grad. 1944

BEGAN STUDYING MUSICAL INSTRUMENT

Roosevelt Elementary School. 1936 (Trombone)
Jr and Sr High School (Trombone)

PRINCIPAL INSTRUMENTAL TEACHERS

Wilson Waite (Elem., Jr and 2 years in High School)
Mr. Bach - 1 year

MUSICAL GROUPS

U.S. Navy Dance Band, Seattle, Wash. 1944
Ashland City Band "I joined many years ago."
Hillah Temple Shrine Band 1958 –
Hillah Temple Shrine German Band 1963 –
Southern Oregon Symphonic Band, Charter Member

MILITARY SERVICE

U.S Navy 1944 - 1947
Farragut Naval Training Station, Idaho. (Electrician)
Lake Union Naval Training Station, Seattle, Wash.
USS FILLMORE APA-83, 4,247-ton Attack Transport

OCCUPATION - PROFESSION

Retail Furniture (GATES FURNITURE MEDFORD/ASHLAND) 1951-82

AT HOME: Talent, Ore. Two children – grown

Charles "Chuck" GEORGE (Drums)

Born: (Glendale, NY) May 28, 1913

Widower

EDUCATION

St. Johns High School and University, Brooklyn, NY.

"I studied law at college two years but it bugged me so I went for my music. I left school at 19."

BEGAN STUDYING INSTRUMENTAL MUSIC

"I was originally interested in music when 8 years old because of my grandpa, Gustav Kapple, who was 1st Clarinet player as well as Violin with John Philip Sousa. Guess I inherited music from my folks. Drums caught my eye and my dad encouraged me. I

Chuck George earned his beans playing in many of the famous bands. He was also a Kay Kyser "look-alike."

started lessons with Buddy Rich – also on vibs."

PRIVATE TEACHERS

Buddy Rich

MUSICAL GROUPS

"I started in the pits with Enoch Light Band in New York. My dad sang with Avon Comedy Four and dad got Ted Weems to hire me in 1948. I stayed with him through middle of 1951 when he closed the Strand Theater in New York as Ted said there was not too much work for 17-piece unit as theaters started dropping stage shows.

"I worked with Mel Torme in Shreveport, then later on with Dick Shawn, also a great guy. I was with Jane Morgan in Milwaukee then Judy Garland and Mickey Rooney (road shows) on the "Hadacol Show." I played with Milton Berle in 'Let Yourself Go.' "

"Ted Weems loaned me $10,000 in 1951 to get on the road playing night clubs and I was able to pay him back in only one year. I worked the first job following Red Nichols in Iroquois Gardens, Louisville, Kentucky. I got booked in 1962 in Portland and stayed there.

"I had the chance to do the "Kay Kyser Story" because I looked like him but turned it down – sorry I did now. He was a nice guy too but I did not want to lip his words as that is rough."

MILITARY SERVICE

U.S. Air Force 2½ years. Discharged in 1944.

OCCUPATION - PROFESSION

Musician. "I joined the union (American Federation of Musicians) when I was 18 in old Local 802 N.Y.C., am now a Life Member.

" I am not really retired, still active on drums and hope to get my own unit again. I had a wonderful group in Portland – four men and two girls singing Andrews Sisters style This sold well and I do mean very well!"

AT HOME: Talent, Oregon. Four children – grown

→ALUM OF THE BAND – RETIRED

Peggie E. GREULING (Alto Saxophone)

Born: (Virginia, Minn.) Oct. 1924
Married: Herbert Greuling 1958

EDUCATION
Northwestern Univ. BS Public School Music, 1946
Univ of Illinois, MS Music Education. 1965

Univ of Maryland	Classes in, German,
Illinois State Univ	Music Education
Univ of Minnesota-Duluth	Music

Conservatory of Music, Wiesbaden, Germany,
Southern Oregon State College, Ashland, Ore.

BEGAN STUDYING INSTRUMENTAL MUSIC
Violin - age 8
Saxophone - age 10
Trumpet - age 13
Viola - age 14
Baritone, Trombone, Tuba

PRINCIPAL INSTRUMENTAL TEACHERS
Glenn Bainum - Northwestern Univ. 1944-46
Vernon Malone - Virginia, Minn.

PRIVATE TEACHERS
Vernon Malone
Willis Coggins
George Dasch
Cecil Leeson

MUSICAL GROUPS
Community Orchestras (11)
City Bands (10)
Ashland City Band, 1970 –
Orchestra for Vienna Ice Revue - 1966
Conservatory Orchestra, Wiesbaden, Germany, 1964-67
School Groups - 35 years
Southern Oregon Symphonic Band, 1991 – 1994 (Retired)

OCCUPATION- PROFESSION
Retired Public School Teacher – Band, Orchestra, Chorus:
Minn., Ill., Wash., Ore., Calif., Fla.
Dept. of Defense High School, Wiesbaden, Germany

HONORS AND AWARDS
"Mrs. Music," Ashland, Ore. 1982

MUSICAL COMPOSITIONS
"In Rogue River valley," 1983;
"Here in Oregon," 1984;
"In Ashland," 1984;
"Pills," 1985;
"My Sheri Jean," 1987;
"Eyes of America," 1990;
"Huggy Bear," 1990;
"High On America," 1993;

AT HOME: Ashland, Ore. Three children – grown

Chris Hald belts it out on his BB♭-Tuba riding on an antique fire truck in a parade. Hald describes himself as an "avid amateur musician."

Christian P. "Chris" HALD M.D. (BB♭ Tuba; String Bass)

Born: (Denmark) Dec. 21, 1920

Married: Jean McCandliss (1944)

EDUCATION

Owatonna High School, Owatonna, Minn.
St. Mary's College, Winona, Minn. (Pre-Med.)
Univ. of Minnesota, BS, BS-Med., M.D. 1952
Infantry OCS, Fort Benning, Ga., 1942
Officer Advanced - Medicine - Fort Sam Houston, Tex.
Officer Advanced - Air Defense Artillery - Fort Bliss, Tex.
U. S. Army Command and general Staff College - Fort Leavenworth, Kan.

BEGAN STUDYING INSTRUMENTAL MUSIC

Owatonna High School - Trombone and Tuba 1936

PRINCIPAL INSTRUMENTAL TEACHERS

Harry Wenger, Owatonna High School 1936-40

Chris Hald in summer 1994.

PRIVATE TEACHERS

Dave Wight, Ashland, Ore. String bass

MUSICAL GROUPS

Owatonna High School Band, 1936-40

Owatonna Elks Club Band, 1936-40

Hillah Temple Shrine Band, Ashland, Ore. 1959 –

Directors: Mr. Cook, Clarence Bell, Irv Mirick, John Drysdale

Southern Oregon Symphonic Band Charter Member

Hillah Temple German Band (1961) Charter Member

Directors: Mr. Cook, Herb Grueling, Raoul Maddox, Harry Kannasto

Fire House Five, 1970 –

Director: Dave Wight

Jester Jolly Boys Dixieland Band, 1968–

Director: Dave Wight

Hillah Saints, 1975 –

Director: Harry Kannasto

Jester Jolly Boy's Band

Director: David Wight

Desperation Seven Dixieland Band, 1980 –

Director: Harry Kannasto

Swing Kings Big band 1987 –

Director: Harry Kannasto

MILITARY SERVICE

Minnesota National Guard Private (Bugler) 1936

World War II - Feb. 10, 1941 - Jan. 21, 1946

Platoon Sergeant, Company "F" 135th Inf, 34th Div. Camp Claiborne, La. Infantry OCS - Fort Benning, Ga. Commissioned 2nd Lt. 3 July, 1942 Camp White, Ore., July 17, 1942, Hq, 91st Div, later 361st Inf. Regt. Promoted to Captain, Commanding Officer Company "I." Commanding this company at Camp White, in Africa, in Italy (European-Middle Eastern Theater of Operations). Discharged as Major. Joined Oregon National guard as Medical Officer; Battalion Surgeon, 2nd Bn, 249th Air Defense Artillery.

Promoted to Lt. Col, commanded medical unit. Promoted to Colonel. Commanded Rear Area Defense Sector. Transferred to Military Hq., Oregon Military Department as "G-1" State Personnel Officer. Retired Aug. 31, 1975.

OCCUPATION - PROFESSION

M.D. Family Practice, Ashland, Ore. 1952-88 (Retired).

Diplomat of American Board of Family Practice; Fellow American Academy of Family Practice.

Author: *Camp White Oregon; The 91st (Fir Tree) Infantry Division.* Webb Research Group Publishers. 1994.

HONORS AND AWARDS

Combat Infantry Badge, 2 Silver Stars for Gallantry, 3 Bronze Stars with V Device for Heroic Achievement, 2 Purple Hearts for wounds, Army Commendation Medal, Presidential Unit Citation, Legion of Merit, 9 other campaign and service medals.

AT HOME Ashland, Ore. Four children – grown

→ALUM OF THE BAND – RETIRED

Bob HANSEN (B*b*-Clarinet)

Born: (Long Beach, Calif.) Aug. 30, 1935

EDUCATION

High School

College.

BEGAN STUDYING INSTRUMENTAL MUSIC

Jacksonville Elementary School, Jacksonville Ore. Steve Whipple

PRINCIPAL INSTRUMENTAL TEACHERS

Steve Whipple, Jacksonville Elementary School 1947

Elmer Ayres, Jacksonville Elementary School 1949

John Eby, Jacksonville Elementary School, 1951

Irv Mirick, Medford High School, 1952-54

John Drysdale, Medford High School, 1952-54

Dr. Smith, Humboldt State College, Arcata, Calif. 1959

PRIVATE TEACHERS

Elmer Ayers

MUSICAL GROUPS

Public and College Bands

Ashland City Band

Southern Oregon Symphonic Band

"I have directed school bands at Noti, Veneta, Medford, and Cascade Christian High School, Medford, Ore."

OCCUPATION - PROFESSION
Public School Teacher – Retired

AT HOME: Medford, Ore.

Nelson Hickling, former "KAZOO" enthusiast, now plays Trumpet.

Nelson Hickling (Trumpet)
Born (Eden, NY) May 27, 1934
Married: Catherine (1989)

EDUCATION
Eden Central School - 1952
Bowling Green State Univ, Bowling Green, Ohio, BS Geology 1957
American Univ. Washington, D.C., MS Geology 1965

BEGAN STUDYING INSTRUMENTAL MUSIC
Age 10, 5th Grade - Trumpet.
My town, Eden, N.Y. is famous as the Home of the "KAZOO" made there since 1916. Many people have told me over the years that they can detect the influence of the "KAZOO" on my tone quality and articulation! I always find that most flattering.

PRINCIPAL INSTRUMENTAL TEACHERS
There were no special teachers in my past. I did not play between ages 23 and 51.
Current teachers in groups I am now in: John Drysdale, Raoul Maddox, Max McKee, Bill Norfleet, Stu Turner, Cindy Hutton

PRIVATE TEACHERS
Rick Emmingswer and Eric Marshall, U.S. Army Band, Washington, D.C. 1986-89
Sam Fowler, Medford, Ore. 1991-92
Larry Hudson, Medford, 1992 –
Have completed two years Music Theory at Southern Oregon State College since retiring.

MUSICAL GROUPS
Two years Air Force ROTC in college, played in ROTC Band.
Damascus, Md. Community Band, 1985-89
Montgomery Village Community Band, 1987-89
Music & Drama Group Band at Goddard Space Center, Greenbelt, Md. 1987-89
Southern Oregon Symphonic Band Charter member, 1989 –
Rogue Valley Wind Ensemble, 1991 –
Southern Oregon State College Jazz Ensemble, 1990 –
Southern Oregon State College Straight Ahead, 1992 –
Medford Music Brass Quintet, 1991 –
Ashland City Band, 1990 –
Hillah Temple German Band, 1989 –
Swing Kings, 1990 –
Jimmy Osgood's Big Band, 1991 –
Brass Group Ensemble/Rogue Valley English Hand Bell Festival
Sheldon James Big Band, 1994 –
Southern Oregon Symphonic Band, 1989 –

OCCUPATION - PROFESSION
Research Geologist -31 years (Retired)

HONORS AND AWARDS
Arion Medal in Instrumental Music (High School), 1952
Music Scholarship Award (High School), 1952
Special Achievement Award, Dept. of the Interior for Geologic Study of the Wind River Indian Reservation, Wyoming, 1978-83

AT HOME: Ashland, Ore. Four children – grown

Randy HUGDAHL (Trombone)
Born: (Chippawa Falls, Wisc.) May 6, 1922
Married: Beverly (1945)

EDUCATION
Riverside High School, Milwaukee, Wisc. 1941

BEGAN STUDYING INSTRUMENTAL MUSIC
High School - trombone

Randy Hugdahl (left) and John Stowe, Trombone "kings."

MUSICAL GROUPS

U. S. Army 91st Infantry Division Band - Camp White, Oregon and in North Africa and Italy.

Ashland City Band

Rack-O-Bones Band

Swing Kings

"Slide Effects"

Randy Hugdahl Quintet

Rogue Valley Wind Ensemble

Hand Bell Festival Brass Sextet

Southern Oregon Symphonic Band Charter Member

MILITARY SERVICE

U. S. Army - 3 Years - 1942-45

"Members of the Band seemed to get a lot of K.P duty, and stood a lot of Guard duty."

OCCUPATION - PROFESSION

U.S. Postal Service. Retired letter carrier - 37 years

HONORS AND AWARDS

European-African-Middle Eastern Theater Medal with 3 Battle Stars; American Theater Medal; Good Conduct Medal; Victory Medal

AT HOME: Medford. Two children – grown

→ALUM OF THE BAND – RETIRED

Frank HUNNICUTT (B♭-Clarinet)
Born: Tulsa, Okla.) July 18, 1934

EDUCATION
3-years college

BEGAN STUDYING INSTRUMENTAL MUSIC
Age 11 - Clarinet in school band
Age 15 - Saxophone

PRIVATE TEACHERS
Harry Kellar, Clarinet, 1950

MUSICAL GROUPS
Many jazz bands - Clarinet, Saxophone
Southern Oregon Symphonic Band – 1994 RETIRED

MILITARY SERVICE
U.S.A.F - 1954-58

OCCUPATION-PROFESSION
Director: Josephine County Building Inspection Dept.

AT HOME Gold Hill, Ore.

→LEAVE OF ABSENCE

Barbara M. HUNT (Bassoon)
Born: (Medford, Ore.) Oct. 28, 1969
Married

EDUCATION
South Medford High School. Grad. 1987
Southern Oregon State College

BEGAN STUDYING INSTRUMENTAL MUSIC
Washington School, Medford, Ore. 5th Grade, Larry Hudson, Clarinet

PRINCIPAL INSTRUMENTAL TEACHERS
McLoughlin Jr. High School, Medford, Ore. Mr. Hansen 1982
McLoughlin Jr. High School, Medford, Ore, Mrs. Bowman 1983
Mid-High School, Medford, Ore., Bob Heide, 1984-85
Senior High School, Medford, Ore., Tom Muller 1986
South Medford High School, Medford, Ore., Bob Heide 1987
Southern Oregon State College. Max McKee 1988-90

PRIVATE TEACHERS
Pat Collins - Clarinet / Bass Clarinet
Cecil Cerines - Bassoon

MUSICAL GROUPS
Southern Oregon Youth Orchestra, 1987
Southern Oregon State College Band, 1988
Southern Oregon State College Alumni Band
Southern Oregon Symphonic Band, 1993 LEAVE

OCCUPATION - PROFESSION
Baker and Banquet Hostess

AT HOME: White City, Ore.

➔ALUM OF THE BAND - RETIRED

Arne S. **JENSEN MD** (Baritone Horn)
Born: (Leavenworth, Wash.) Dec. 27, 1918
Married: Helene 1987

EDUCATION
Monmouth High School, Monmouth, Ore. Grad. 1935
Oregon Normal School, Monmouth, Ore. Teaching Certificate
Univ. of Oregon, BS - returned in 1939 – premed 1943
Univ. of Oregon Medical School. MD 1945

BEGAN STUDYING INSTRUMENTAL MUSIC
Jr. High School - Mellophone, 1931

MUSICAL GROUPS
Oregon Normal School, Orchestra. Mellophone (Floyd Ellefson)

MUSICAL GROUPS
Southern Oregon Symphonic Band, 1992 - 1994 RETIRED

MILITARY SERVICE
U. S. Naval Reserve. 6 years as Medical Doctor. Served in U.S., completed
Residency then in Navy V- 1 2 program, assigned to
VA Hospital at American Lake, Tacoma, Wash. 194748.

HONORS AND AWARD
Chief of Staff, Albany General Hospital, Albany, Ore.
President Linn County Medical Society
Chief of Staff, McKenzie-Willamette Hospital, Springfield, Ore.

OCCUPATION-PROFESSION
Taught Elementary schools in Valsetz (1 year), Hillsboro (1 year)

Medical Doctor. Private Practice Albany, and Eugene, Ore. 16 years.
Medical Director for Weyerhaeuser Timber Co., Springfield, Ore, 2 years.

"I returned to Private Practice in Springfield, Ore. in 4-doctor medical group, 8 years. Set up first full-time Emergency Room and was its Director in McKenzie-Willamette Hospital, Springfield, Ore. in 1972. Retired, moved to Oregon coast but returned to work as part-time physician at Waldport, Ore. Retired – 1987."

AT HOME: Medford, Ore. 5 children – grown

Sharon JAMES (Flute)

Born: (Ashland, Ore.) December, 21, 1951
Married: Bill James (1971)

EDUCATION
Phoenix High School, Phoenix, Ore. Grad. 1970
Southern Oregon State College, BA-Music Education, 1974
University of Oregon, (3 summers)

BEGAN STUDYING INSTRUMENTAL MUSIC
Bellview Elementary School, Ashland, flute, 5th and 6th grades.
Ashland Jr. High School
Phoenix High School

PRINCIPAL INSTRUMENTAL TEACHERS
Frank Kenney, Ashland Public Schools
Gary Monical, Phoenix High School
Max McKee, Southern Oregon State College

PRIVATE TEACHERS
Phebe Kimball

MUSICAL GROUPS
Southern Oregon State College Alumni Band
State of Jefferson Sometimes Marching Band - 9 years
Upper Rogue Community Band
A-B-C Director's Band
Southern Oregon Symphonic Band 1993–

OCCUPATION - PROFESSION
Telephone sales Rep., Jackson & Perkins - Bear Creek Corp.

AT HOME: Talent, Ore. Two children – teens
"Native of the Rogue River Valley"

HEBRIDES SUITE
Airs from Marjory Kennedy-Fraser's Collection "Songs of the Hebrides"
CLARE GRUNDMAN

Sheldon JAMES (Alto Saxophone)

Born: (Cleveland, Ohio) Apr. 25, 1926

Married: Diane VanBrocklin James (1978)

EDUCATION

Euclid Central High School, Euclid, Ohio

Miami University, Oxford, Ohio (3 years)

BEGAN STUDYING INSTRUMENTAL MUSIC

First instrument: Violin. High School orchestra 1942-43

Second instrument: Alto Saxophone. 1943

Third instrument: Clarinet 1943

PRINCIPAL INSTRUMENTAL TEACHERS

Miami University Concert Orchestra. (Clarinet) Harry Peters, Cond.

MUSICAL GROUPS

Miami University Concert Orchestra

"My entire music career has been with jazz and dance bands. I toured with jazz violinist Joe Venuti, the bands of singers Ray Eberle, Russ Carlyle, etc. Played in backup bands for Four Freshmen, Dorothy Dandridge, Gogi Grant, etc."

Southern Oregon Symphonic Band 1992–

OCCUPATION - PROFESSION

Business forms - Distributor (retired)

Musician

AT HOME: Ashland, Ore. Two children – grown

Harry R. KANNASTO (Trumpet)

Born: (Ashland, Ore.) Oct. 29, 1930

Married: Shirley (1952)

EDUCATION

Ashland, Ore. High School Grad. 1948

University of Oregon, 1948-49

Southern Oregon State College BA 1952

Southern Oregon State College MA 1961

BEGAN STUDYING INSTRUMENTAL MUSIC

Ashland schools, "I started to play Cornet in 3rd Grade under Ward Croft, class band teacher.

Other teachers: Gordon Tripp 1940-41

Irv Mirick 1942-45; Jack Francis, 1946; Irv Lesser 1947-48

PRIVATE TEACHERS

Ward Croft, Irv Mirick, Irv Lesser, Byron Miller, Ira Lee

Volunteers of the Symphonic Band played for Memorial Day service in Ashland's Mountain View Cemetery. A blustery, rainy day, Hugh Littlebury (drummer) played "umbrella" as Harry Kannasto directed.

MUSICAL GROUPS

Hillah Temple Shrine Band - 30 years (Directors: Charles Cook, Clarence Bell, Irv Mirick, Raoul Maddox, Chuck Mason, John Drysdale)

Ashland, Ore. City Band - 43 seasons: Directors, Irv Mirick*, Dr. Glenn Matthews, Charles Cook (CWO), Dr. Herbert Cecil, Dave Wight, Raoul Maddox*

Hillah Temple German Band - 28 years (Director)

Hillah Temple Shrine Saints Dixieland Combo - 10 years

Desperation Seven - 5 years

Swing Kings Big Dance Band - 8 years (Director - Trumpet)

Southern Oregon State College Wind Ensemble, 1988 –

Southern Oregon Symphonic Band - Charter Member

Rogue Valley Brass Choir - 3 years

Rogue Valley Wind Ensemble - 6 years

Hand Bell Festival Brass Sextet

"I am currently Director of the *Hillah* Temple Shrine Band; Shrine German Band; Shrine Swing Kings Big Band; Brass Group Ensemble."

---

* We were offered Sectional Technique Lessons but numerous times when I was the only one to show up, these turned out to be private lessons.

MILITARY SERVICE

Served with Hq. Battery, Oregon Army National Guard, Ashland, 1948-1957. (Staff Sergeant)

(Top) Harry Kannasto sounds "To the Colors" at Veterans Administration Domiciliary Concert Sept. 24, 1994. (Lower) Always smiling Kannasto.

OCCUPATION - PROFESSION

Phoenix-Talent Schools. Elementary and High School Bands and Choirs. 1952-1969

Medford Schools. Elementary and Junior High School Bands 1969-1986.

HONORS – PROFESSION

Listed in *American College Student Leaders,* 1952

Theta Delta Phi Ed. Honorary.; Student Council; SOSC Football, Little All-Coast Selection; All-Conference Scholastic Scholarship; *Phi Delta Kappa* - Ed. Masters Honorary.

AT HOME: Ashland, Ore. One child – grown

Duke McQueen, Lowell Anderson, Bill Laurine, beat drums and crash cymbals during a Shrine Band outing to San Francisco.

Zerald Wm. "Bill" LAURINE (Bass Drum / Cymbals)

Born: Lincoln, Neb. Nov. 15, 1920

Married: Dora May "Dode" Laurine

EDUCATION

Elementary Schools, Enumclaw, Renton, Bryn Mawr, Black Diamond, Wash.

Black Diamond High School. Grad. 1939

BEGAN STUDYING INSTRUMENTAL MUSIC

Age 6, "My introduction to rhythm keeping time with fiddle players that practiced at my home in Enumclaw. As a young teenager I went to band practice once a week, six miles hike round trip. I never had any lessons on the drums. "

MUSICAL GROUPS

Afife Shrine Band, Tacoma and Shrine Band in Seattle as teenager.

Enumclaw City Band.

Ashland City Band, 1949

Hillah Temple Shrine Band, 1949 –

Southern Oregon Symphonic Band Charter Member

MILITARY SERVICE

U. S. Army Signal Corps.; Camp Crowder, Mo.

U S. Army Air Force. Dispatcher, Base Operations, Orlando, Fla.

Served in England. Landed at Omaha Beach on D+2; set up Advanced Landing Fields for P-47 fighter planes advancing across Europe with the war.

OCCUPATION - PROFESSION

Founded Laurine's Carpet House and Rug Barn, Medford, 1953.

Retired 1991.

AT HOME. Medford. Two children – grown

Hugh Littlebury

Hugh LITTLEBURY (Drums & Bells)

Born: (Detroit, Mich.) Apr. 5, 1920

Married: Marie (1982)

EDUCATION

St. John's Military Academy (High School), Delafield, Wisc. 1939

Michigan State College, Engineering and Science.

"I left college in 1941, after two years, due to World War II. Later, went to several schools studying Electric Engineering in Michigan and California.

BEGAN STUDY INSTRUMENTAL MUSIC

Piano at age 9.

PRINCIPAL INSTRUMENTAL TEACHERS

George Shulte, Jr. (Violin in Concert Orchestras)

MUSICAL GROUPS

"I was in Concert Orchestra at Age 12. Started my own Dance Orchestra with some of the Concert Musicians at age 15. Went to Military Academy (age 17) played Piano.

"Started an 18-piece Orchestra at Michigan State College in 1939, played many college and out-of-town functions until band broke up with start of the war, when members went into the military.

"Played with Lou Waters after we met in the Pacific war zone. We put a band together then played in Naval bases in Hawaiian Islands, 1944-46."

Southern Oregon Symphonic Band, 1993 –

MILITARY SERVICE

U. S. Navy 1941 - 1953 (Chief Petty Officer)

"After World War II, I joined the Naval Reserve and was recalled for the Korean War. Stationed in Philippines. Back in U.S., I operated the Fleet Airborne Electronics–Pacific at North Island, Calif. Declined full Commander rank in 1953 to be a family man and rear our son and daughter. Left Navy and joined Rohr Aircraft, Riverside; later Aeroquip in Burbank.

OCCUPATION - PROFESSION

Retired. Electrical Engineer. "In 1944, at Kelvinator Refrigerator, I helped design the first two "Temperature Refrigerators" that permitted both a freezer and refrigerator from the same compressor in the same cabinet."

AT HOME: Medford. Two children (first marriage)– grown
Three children - adopted (second marriage) - grown

Kathleen MACKRIS (Oboe)

Born: (Cleveland, Ohio) Nov. 28, 1957
Married: Steve Groveman 1984

EDUCATION

Maple Heights High School - Maple Heights Ohio. Grad. 1975
Chatham College, Pittsburgh, Pa. BA Philosophy/Political Science 1980

BEGAN STUDYING INSTRUMENTAL MUSIC

Elementary School, Maple Heights, (near Cleveland) Ohio - (Flute)
Junior and Senior High: Oboe

PRIVATE TEACHERS

Arthur Stefano, Cleveland Orchestra.
Randy Isreal (San Francisco)
Glenn Matthews, Ashland, Ore.

MUSICAL GROUPS

High School Bands
Shaker Symphony, Oberlin, Ohio
Community Women's Orchestra, San Francisco, Calif.
Southern Oregon Symphonic Band 1994 –

OCCUPATION- PROFESSION

Real Estate Appraiser Owns: ROGUE APPRAISERS, Medford, Ore.

AT HOME: Ashland. Two children ages 6 and 8.

→ALUM OF THE BAND – RETIRED

James M. "Jim" MACY (Trumpet)
Born: (Fairfield, Iowa) Sept. 30, 1914

EDUCATION
(Not listed)

BEGAN STUDYING INSTRUMENTAL MUSIC
1985 - Rudy Domitrovich, Trumpet

PRIVATE TEACHERS
Rudy Domitrovich
Warren Moore

MUSICAL GROUPS
Southern Oregon Men's Band, Raoul Maddox, Dir., 1985
Southern Oregon Symphonic Band, Charter Member –Retired 1992

MILITARY SERVICE
U.S. Navy 1942-

OCCUPATION- PROFESSION
Sears, Roebuck Co., Credit Manager - 25 years (Retired)

AT HOME: Ashland, Ore.

Gary MALONE (Trombone)
Born: (Long Beach, Calif.) Mar. 29, 1957
Married: Darlene 1979

EDUCATION
Ashland High School, Grad. 1975
Southern Oregon State College, 1979-81
Rogue Community College (Applied Sciences)

BEGAN STUDYING INSTRUMENTAL MUSIC
Sequoia Jr High School, Reseda, Calif, 1969

PRINCIPAL INSTRUMENTAL TEACHERS
Gerald Winters, Sequoia Jr. High School Band, 1969
Gerald Winters, Sequoia Jr. High School Orchestra, 1970-71
Raoul Maddox, Ashland High School, Band/Brass Quartet, 1974-54

MUSICAL GROUPS
School Bands
Central Point City Jazz Band 1984-85

MILITARY SERVICE
U.S. Navy, Norfolk, Va. Boiler Tech. 3rd Class – 1975-81
Oregon Army National Guard (SP4) 1981-83

OCCUPATION-PROFESSION
Power Plant Operator

AT HOME: Eagle Point, Ore. Three Children: 1, 11, 15

Harry MARSHALL (Trumpet)
Born: (Medford, Ore.) Sept. 29, 1960

EDUCATION
Washington, Roosevelt Elementary Schools, Medford, Ore.
Medford Sr. High School - Grad 1978.
Real Estate School, 1978. Certificate
Southern Oregon State College 1979-81
Oregon State College, 1981
University of Oregon, 1981-84

BEGAN STUDYING INSTRUMNENTAL MUSIC
Piano - 1968
Trumpet, 1971 Medford Schools

PRINCIPAL INSTRUMENTAL TEACHERS
Kenneth Raymond (Piano)
Roosevelt Elementary School - Ron Bartlett, Harry Kannasto
Hedrick Jr. High School - Ron Bartlett, Harry Kannasto
Medford Mid High School - Robert Bork, Robert Heide
Medford Sr. High School - Band, Stage Band, Pep Band - Tom Muller, Larry Hudson; Orchestra, John Drysdale

MUSICAL GROUPS
Oregon State College. Jazz Band II
University of Oregon, Marching Band, Concert Band
Southern Oregon State College Symphonic Wind Ensemble
Hat Band.
Southern Oregon Symphonic Band 1991 –

OCCUPATION - PROFESSION
Real Estate Broker, Medford. Ore.)

AT HOME: Medford, Ore.

Jeannette MARSHALL (Flute)
Born: (Portland, Ore.) Mar. 10, 1921
Widow: Harry B. Marshall, Sr. (d. 1991)

EDUCATION
Medford Senior High School, Medford, Ore. Grad. 1938
Southern Oregon Normal School, Ashland 1938-40
Pre-law Certificate
University of Oregon Law School, 1941-43, LL.B.
University of Minnesota Law School 1946, LL.M.

BEGAN STUDYING MUSICAL INSTRUMENTS
Lincoln School, Medford, 1929. Wilson Waite, Flute
Jr. High - Sr. High Schools, Band - Orchestra, Wilson Waite

PRINCIPAL INSTRUMENTAL TEACHERS
Wilson Waite 1929-34
William Bolger 1936-38
Lucy Landen, (Southern Oregon Normal School) 1939-40 Flute, Violin; Orchestra Direction

MUSICAL GROUPS
Southern Oregon Symphony 1943, 1946, ?-1958
Univ. of Oregon Law School Band, 1943
Rogue Valley Symphony, Richard Werner, Cond.
Southern Oregon Symphonic Band, 1993–

OCCUPATION - PROFESSION
Attorney.
→"Starting my second 50 years – Not retired!

"Jeanette [Thatcher] Marshall became the first woman associate in a Portland law firm after graduation from the University of Oregon Law School in 1943. At U of O she was one of three women law students and the only one to graduate. Her graduating class had just three people. She opened her office in Medford in 1944,

Jeannette Marshall (right) led the Univ. of Oregon Law School "Marching Band" in 1943. Fifty years later she is still a lawyer, still plays flute and loves both.

was one of only 25 lawyers in town." [—Oregon State Bar *Bulletin*, June 1994. p.37] There are presently 200 lawyers in Medford, and 275 in Jackson County. For the first 30 years of my practice, I was the only woman lawyer in the county."

HONORS AND AWARDS
Univ of Oregon Plaque: Top Law School Student – Class of 1943.
Oregon State Bar Ass'n Certificate: 50-years of Law Practice – 1993

AT HOME: Medford. Two children – grown

Glenn MATTHEWS Ph.D. (Oboe - English Horn)
Born: (Boston, Mass.) Sept. 3, 1913
Married: Kathleen Jones 1956

EDUCATION
High School: San Jose, Calif.
San Jose State College
University of Oregon, MA, 1957; Ph.D. 1974
(Dissertation: *The Teaching of Conducting in U. S. Colleges.*)

BEGAN STUDYING INSTRUMENTAL MUSIC
1920 – with parents
High School Band and Orchestra (Oboe)

PRINCIPAL INSTRUMENTAL TEACHERS
Band: Tom Eagan (WW Ensemble)
Dad: George T. Matthews – San Jose State College

Univ. of California - Berkeley, Charles Cushing, Dir, (band)
Gustave

PRIVATE TEACHERS
George T. Matthews (father)
C. Addimando (San Francisco Symphony 1930)

MUSICAL GROUPS
Many chamber groups
San Jose Bands and Orchestras
Univ of California (Berkeley) Band and Symphony, 1935
Modesto Symphony, 1942-45
Carmel Bach Festival (5 years)
Medford Philharmonic Orchestra 1946-56 (Oboe)
Rogue Valley Symphony (Espec. English Horn)
Ashland City Band 35 years - (Director 1946-51)
Southern Oregon Symphonic Band Charter Member

OCCUPATION- PROFESSION
Professor of Music, Southern Oregon State College
Jazz Quartet member - leader
Employee/Faculty Jazz Quarter (member - leader)
Many private pupils especially Oboe
Chairman: Mt. Ashland Men's Garden Club
Compositions:
"Citation," "Festival" (Concert Marches)
Tone Poem: "Biorama" for Oboe and strings
Trio: Oboe, Violin, Clarinet
Arranger: Oboe solo and band: The Little Shepherd"(Debussy)
Oboe and Organ: "Priere" (Boelhmann)
Many jazz combo and chamber group arrangements
"Upbeats" Jazz Quarter, 1950-65

AT HOME: Ashland, Ore. (since Aug. 1946) Two children – grown

Irv Mirick's application picture (left) for his first teaching job. As *Director Emeritus* (right) of Shrine and Southern Oregon Symphonic Bands in 1994.

→ALUM OF THE BAND – RETIRED

Irving A. "Irv" MIRICK

Director Emeritus & Musician Extraordinary

Born: (Huron, S.Dak.) Jan. 7, 1910
Married: Naomi Smith (1931) (1906 - 1990)

EDUCATION

Amamosa High School, Amamosa, Iowa Grad. 1927
Upper Iowa Univ., Fayette, Iowa. BA Physical Ed and Biology. 1931.
"I had only one music class as an undergraduate. I always regretted not having more, for when I decided to go to Graduate School in Music, I had to back up and take all those music prep courses that I'd missed. These took me an extra year."
Univ. of Iowa MA Music. 1939

BEGAN STUDYING INSTRUMENTAL MUSIC

Trumpet with father, 1927
Piano with mother, about 1925-27
Hermie Voxman, Clarinet.
Modeste Allo, Trombone
Ira Lee, Bass

Snapshot:
(left to right) Bert Webber, Baritone Horn, John Drysdale, Director, Irv Mirick, former Director and timpanist. All three were teachers at Medford Sr. High School in 1969, had reunion in Southern Oregon Symphonic Band in 1993.

PRINCIPAL INSTRUMENTAL TEACHERS

Dr. Philip Greeley Clapp, Dean of Music School, Univ. of Iowa, (Orchestra) 1936-1939 – Trumpet
Charles Righter, Univ. of Iowa, Band, 1936-39 – Trumpet

PRIVATE TEACHERS

Modeste Allo
Hermie Voxman

MUSICAL GROUPS

Iowa Univ., Symphony Orchestra, 1936-39 (summers) Trumpet
Iowa Univ., Dance Bands, Trumpet
City Summer Bands: Keota and Amamosa, Iowa; Ashland, Ore.
Hillah Temple Shrine Band (Director)
Southern Oregon Symphonic Band (Director - 1 year)
Timpani 1993 – Retired 1994

OCCUPATION - PROFESSION

"My first year of teaching was at Kinross, Iowa, a little farm town with a population of 175. There were about 70 in the High School. I was hired right out of college to be Principal, Math and Social Studies teacher. I also had the baseball and basketball teams. One day, I announced that all the students would assemble and we would try out band instruments. I formed a small band, and we went on into the state championships, finishing near the top.

"I moved to Ashland, Oregon to teach band in the Elementary School as well as at the college. Both schools were part of the same contract. This was 1942-45. The Normal school during World War-II only had two buildings. There were 75 students – all girls except one boy who was a 4-F Draft Classification so he did not qualify for the

Army. Oh, but all those girls made him miserable. He played Trombone.

"I moved to Medford schools in 1945 and retired there in 1974. I went from Band teacher to become Director of Instrumental Music, Medford, Ore. School Dist. 549C, and was in that school district for 29 years."

Irv Mirick, a champion of instrumental band music, trained thousands of young people. One, who studied with him nearly 25 years ago wrote, "...he made a lasting impression on my life."

Hillah Temple Shrine Band (Director) 20 years

Southern Oregon Symphonic Band, Charter Member (Director) 1 year

AT HOME: Medford, Ore. One child – grown

Preston MITCHELL (BB*b*- Tuba)

Born: (Homer, Mich.) Sept. 4, 1917

Married: Cora. 1942 d.1992

Mitchell started with Clarinet, moved to Tuba

EDUCATION

Whittier, Calif. High School. Grad. 1935

Whittier College. AA, Music; AB, Music, 1946

Archer School of Photography, 1948

BEGAN STUDYING INSTRUMENTAL MUSIC

Junior High School - Whittier - Clarinet

PRINCIPAL INSTRUMENTAL TEACHERS

Fullerton Junior College, Mr. Wallberg. String bass, 1935-37; Whittier College. Mr. Haroldson. 1938-40

PRIVATE TEACHERS: Spike Wallace (President of Local 47 in LA - played Tuba in LA Philharmonic and in Hollywood Studios) String Bass and Tuba

MUSICAL GROUPS

Whittier College Orchestra

Rio Honda Symphony

Air Force Band, March Field, Calif.

Taught Instrumental Music in elementary schools

Hand Bell Festival Brass Sextet

Southern Oregon Symphonic Band, 1991—

MILITARY SERVICE

U.S. Air Force bands -3½ years. Bugler on Okinawa.

OCCUPATION - PROFESSION

Foster & Kleiser, North American.

Commercial Photographer, 35 years

AT HOME: Medford, Ore. Two children – grown

Preston Mitchell plays his Tuba under "rain-strainer" during 1993 Memorial Day Service at Mountain View Cemetery. Home practice (right) in fall 1994.

→LEAVE OF ABSENCE

Maurice "Mickey" MORELLI (French Horn)

Born: (Orange, N.J.) Dec. 9, 1917

Married: Evelyn

EDUCATION

Bloomfield High School, Bloomfield, N.J. Grad 1937
Radio and radar Schools, U.S. Army Air Force 1942-44
ICS Radio-Electronic School 1946-48
CREI Radio-Electronic School, 1948-49
Spokane Music Conservatory, Spokane, Wash., 1950-51
Orchestration, Harmony, Composition

BEGAN STUDYING INSTRUMENTAL MUSIC

Piano, Edward Habig, Newark, N.J.
Organ
French Horn, in Air Force Band pending discharge

PRIVATE TEACHERS

Edward Habig, Newark, N.J.

MUSICAL GROUPS
Spokane Symphony 1945-1958
San Diego County Symphony (various periods until 1985)
San Diego Jewish Community Orchestra, David Amos, Dir., 1963-1985
Mesa College (and other school groups)
Swing Kings - Piano
Southern Oregon Symphonic Band – 1994 RETIRED

MILITARY SERVICE
Air Force, 1942-45 Radio, Radar, Gunner B-24 bomber, Pacific Theater.
"31 completed missions over Truk, Caroline Islands"

OCCUPATION - PROFESSION
Electronic Technician, Spokane, Wash. 1945-1958
Electronic Engineering, San Diego, Calif. 1987 until Retirement

HONORS AND AWARDS
Military: Asiatic-Pacific Theater Medal
American Theater Medal, Victory Medal

AT HOME: Gold Hill, Ore

"Duke" McQueen, Drummer

Stuart V. "Duke" McQUEEN (Drums)

Born: (Portland, Ore.) Jan. 7, 1920

Married: Margaret McQueen (1943)

EDUCATION

Washington High School, Portland. Grad. 1937

Oregon State College. BS Business. 1943

Member: *SAE* Fraternity

BEGAN STUDYING INSTRUMENTAL MUSIC

Hillah Temple Shrine Band - Snare Drum, 1958

PRINCIPAL INSTRUMENTAL TEACHERS

Mostly self-taught (no formal training) with help from fellow Shriners: Bill Abbott, Milo Kubalek, Bill Laurine, Irv Mirick

MUSICAL GROUPS

Hillah Temple Shrine Band 1958 –

Hillah Temple German Band

Ashland Elks Kilty Band

Lausmann's Lousy Loggers, 12 years

Southern Oregon Symphonic Band, Charter Member

MILITARY SERVICE

U. S. Army. Captain, Infantry Reserves, Tank Destroyer Commander.

Japan Occupation Force (31 months).

R.O.T.C. (Oregon State College)

OCCUPATION - PROFESSION

Formerly President, CEO, KOGAP MANUFACTURING COMPANY - 46 years. Retired Dec. 31, 1992.

AT HOME: Medford, Ore. Four children – grown

Jodi O'CONNELL (Flute)

Born: (Green Bay, Wisc.) June 12, 1967

EDUCATION

Jordan High School, Jordan, Iowa

Luther College, Decorah, Iowa

BEGAN STUDYING INSTRUMENTAL MUSIC

Piano - age 3

Various woodwinds and percussion – self-taught, starting about age 12

PRINCIPAL INSTRUMENTAL TEACHERS
Nancy Kopperud, piano and organ
Flute: self-taught, but attended music camps and flute workshops

MUSICAL GROUPS
High School Bands
Luther College Concert Band
Southern Oregon Symphonic Band, 1993 –
Southern Oregon Wind Ensemble
Ashland City Band

OCCUPATION - PROFESSION
Private piano and woodwind instructor

AT HOME: Phoenix, Ore.

Jean POWELL (Baritone Saxophone)
Born: (Sacramento, Calif.) Feb. 5, 1955
Married: David Powell (1983)

EDUCATION
Foothills High School, Sacramento, Calif. Grad. 1973
American River Jr. College
Sacramento State Univ. BA Media Communications, 1978
College of Marin
Southern Oregon State College

BEGAN STUDYING INSTRUMENTAL MUSIC
"I bought a $100 Alto Saxophone in 1976 and proceeded to take lessons. I now have a "Sax" family owning Soprano, Alto, Tenor, Baritone, C-melody."

PRINCIPAL INSTRUMENTAL TEACHERS
College of Marin, Calif. Staff teachers.

PRIVATE TEACHERS
Mike Vannice, Randy Magnelenus, Jan Jaseau

MUSICAL GROUPS
"My first band experience was at College of Marin where I took Symphonic and Jazz band. That was in 1980. I was in a Rock-n-Roll Band for one year in San Francisco. We played two gigs at the Haight Street Fair, then at a bar in Sebastipol, Calif."
Southern Oregon Wind Ensemble
Southern Oregon State College Symphonic Band, 1991 –
Al Terras Band, Grants Pass
Southern Oregon Symphonic Band 1993 –

OCCUPATION - PROFESSION
Telephone Order Entry Clerk, Harry & David, Medford, Ore.

AT HOME: Jacksonville, Ore. Children: "1st child in the making!"

John PURCELL (French Horn)
Born: (Portland, Ore.) Nov. 18, 1920
Married, Nadine 1962

EDUCATION
West Linn High School, West Linn, Ore. Grad. 1938
Oregon College of Education (now WOSC) Ed. 1946
University of California (Berkeley) M.L.S. 1966

BEGAN STUDYING INSTRUMENTAL MUSIC
Piano about age 8 (Mother)
Trumpet - High School 1934, changed to Baritone 1935
French Horn - Univ. of Oregon 1938

PRINCIPAL INSTRUMENTAL TEACHERS
Fred Wade, West Linn High School 1934-38
John Stehn, Univ. of Oregon 1938-39
Jack Shields (CWO) 162nd Inf. Regt, Oregon National Guard 1938-41

MUSICAL GROUPS
Syracuse University Marching Band, 1943
Hillah Temple Shrine Band, 1966 –
Southern Oregon Symphonic Band, Charter Member
Culver, Ore. High School Band (Director) 1946-47

MILITARY SERVICE
U.S. Army 162nd Infantry Band, Fort Lewis, Wash. 1940-41
Director and Commanding Officer, 55th Army Band, Nara, Japan, 1949-50,
Various posts, including 8 months in Europe, 1942-45
Infantry (Lt.) U. S. and Japan, 1949-53

OCCUPATION - PROFESSION
Librarian - Southern Oregon State College (Retired)

AT HOME: Ashland, Ore.

→LEAVE OF ABSENCE

Cynthia RAYMOND (Flute)
Born: (Detroit, Mich.) Mar. 16, 1939
Married: Burke Raymond

EDUCATION
Northville High School, Northville, Mich.
In college: B.M. and R.N.

BEGAN STUDYING INSTRUMENTAL MUSIC
Piano, age 6
Dance - classical ballet, age 7
Flute, age 12

PRIVATE TEACHERS
David Eagle - Minnesota
Jane Bowers - Portland, Ore.
Martha Herby - Portland, Ore.

MUSICAL GROUPS
Beaverton Chamber Orchestra
Marylhurst College Symphony
Musical Offering
Southern Oregon Symphonic Band

OCCUPATION - PROFESSION
Registered Nurse
Music teacher / performer ("Toot Sweet)

AT HOME: Jacksonville, Ore.

Sylvia SCHMELING (Alto Saxophone)
Born: (Ladysmith, Wisc.) May 11, 1936
Married: Herman Schmeling (1959)

EDUCATION
Ladysmith High School. Grad. 1953
Univ. of Wisconsin, Whitewater, Wisc. BS, Business Educ. 1958
Southern Oregon State College, Ashland, Ore. MS, Education - Reading Specialist 1972

BEGAN STUDYING INSTRUMENTAL MUSIC
Ladysmith High School, Ed. Svare
Univ. of Wisconsin, Whitewater, John Bushnell
Ashland City Band, Raoul Maddox

PRIVATE TEACHERS
Mrs. Armstrong, Ladysmith, Wisc.

MUSICAL GROUPS
Ladysmith High School Bands: Concert, Jazz
Rogue Valley Symphony, 1985
College Bands: Concert, Pep
Ashland City Band, 1977 –
Southern Oregon Symphonic Band, 1994 –

Sylvia Schmeling – now and earlier.

OCCUPATION - PROFESSION
Retired Teacher:
1st Grade, Jr. High Schools
Technical Vocational School – (Post-High School), Eau Claire, Wisc.
—"plus 10 years as a Reading Specialist"

AT HOME: Ashland, Ore. Three children – grown

William "Bill" SHACKELFORD (E*b* & BB*b* Sousaphone)
Born: (San Francisco, Calif.) Aug. 22, 1925
Married: Loretta (1960)

EDUCATION
Public Schools, Yreka, Calif. 1943
Univ. of Southern California. 1948-51
Central Washington College of Education
314th College Training Detachment, USAF - Pre-flight Aeronautics

BEGAN STUDYING INSTRUMENTAL MUSIC
Started in Elementary School, 1934, Prof. A. F. Galgano, (E*b*-Tuba)
Finished 1943, Prof. A. F. Galgano.

Bill Shackelford today with Sousaphone (left), and as a student with Tuba that was bigger than he was.

PRINCIPAL INSTRUMENTAL TEACHERS
Prof. Galgano
USC Marching Band, Thomas Thompson - 10 days.

PRIVATE TEACHERS
Mrs. Ruth Galgano, Piano

MUSICAL GROUPS
USAF CTD Band 1943-44 (4 months) (BB♭-Tuba)
Southern Oregon Symphonic Band 1992

MILITARY SERVICE
U. S. Air Force 1943-46

OCCUPATION - PROFESSION
Motor Transportation. Driver, Supervisor, Company owner

AT HOME: Jacksonville, Oregon. Two children – grown

Robert SCHOLL (E♭-Tuba)
Born: (Beaverton, Ore.) Jan. 14, 1947
Married: Kathryn (1980)

EDUCATION
Klamath Union High School. Grad. 1965
Reed College, Portland, Ore. Political Science 1969
Univ. of Oregon Law School. JD. 1975

BEGAN STUDYING INSTRUMENTAL MUSIC
Riverside School 4th Grade, Klamath Falls, Mr. Whalen - 1958

PRINCIPAL INSTRUMENTAL TEACHERS
Normand Poulshock, Fremont Jr. High School, Klamath Falls, Ore.
Lamar Jensen, Klamath Union High School

MUSICAL GROUPS
Just Call Me Squirt, Eugene, Ore. (Electric Bass) 1973
New Mime Circus Theater Ensemble, Eugene, Ore. 1977
Ashland City Band 1989
Southern Oregon Symphonic Band, 1988

OCCUPATION – PROFESSION
Fund raising Consultant

AT HOME: Ashland, Ore. Two children, young teens

Charles Shuttle in the late 1940's when he was in the United States Marine Band.

Charles SHUTTLE (Tenor Saxophone)
Born: (Pasadena, Calif.) Sept. 19, 1927
Married: Maryke Shuttle (1986)

EDUCATION
East High School, Denver, Colo. Grad. 1945
Univ. of Maryland, BS Electrical Engineering. 1954

BEGAN STUDYING INSTRUMENTAL MUSIC
At age 8, Trumpet. 1935.
At age 14 switched to Baritone Horn
Saxophone, 1987

MUSICAL GROUPS
U. S. Marine Band, Washington, D.C. 1948-1950
Southern Oregon State College Band, 1990-92
Southern Oregon Symphonic Band 1989–

MILITARY SERVICE
U.S. Marine Corps 1946-1950 Served in Nevada, San Francisco Naval Shipyard, Washington, D.C.
U.S. Maritime Service, Chief Yeoman.

OCCUPATION - PROFESSION
Electrical-Mechanical Reliability Engineer (Retired)

AT HOME: Ashland, Ore. One child – grown

Catherine Jeannette SLEPPY (Bassoon)
Born: (Tucson, Ariz.) May 21, 1954

EDUCATION
Eureka Sr. High School, Eureka, Calif. Grad. 1972
Humboldt State Univ., Arcata, Calif. 1977
Bartlesville Wesleyan Bible College, Bartlesville, Okla.

BEGAN STUDYING INSTRUMENTAL MUSIC
4th Grade at Worthington Elem. School, Eureka, Calif.
Jr. High School
Eureka High School
Humboldt State University

PRINCIPAL INSTRUMENTAL TEACHERS
Don Moehenke, Gerald Davies (Elem. school)
Bob Armstrong (Jr. High School)
Jim Westman (High School)
Charles Fulkerson, orchestra
Val Phillips, Bob Cockran, band

PRIVATE TEACHERS
Les Weil, Bob Cockran, David Gordon, Phil Kates (oboe)

MUSICAL GROUPS
All City Honor Band (elem. school)
All County Honor Band (high school)

The Jester Hairston Concert (Dir. by Jester Hairston)
Chamber groups - Humboldt State Univ.
Humboldt Light Symphony
Redding Symphony, Redding, Calif.
Siskiyou Community College Orchestra
Royal County Theater Orchestra
Rogue Community Theater: "Oklahoma," "Music Man," "South Pacific," "Carrousel," "Camelot"
Rogue Opera, "Magic Flute"
Rogue Valley Symphony Orchestra (Cond. Roger Dicky, Y. Straus, Art Shaw, Mela Meta (Guest Conductor)
Southern Oregon Symphonic Band 1994–
Choir: Eureka High School,
Humboldt State Univ.,
Bartlesville Wesleyan Bible College

OCCUPATION - PROFESSION

Child Care
Church Christmas and Easter programs. Escorts church vocal groups on tours

AT HOME: Medford

John SLEPPY (F-BB*b*- Tuba)

Born: (San Francisco, Calif.) Jan. 12, 1949

EDUCATION

Eureka Sr. High School - Eureka, Calif. Grad 1967
Humboldt State Univ. Arcata, Calif. BA Music; Teaching Cert. 1972

BEGAN STUDYING INSTRUMENTAL MUSIC

"My first teacher was my father, Walter Sleppy. Started in 4th grade."

PRINCIPAL INSTRUMENTAL TEACHERS

Elementary School - Don Mochenke
Jr. High School - Bob Armstrong
High School - Louis Weichselfelder
College Band - Valsire Philips; -Orchestra, Charles Fulkerson, choir, Dr. Barlow

PRIVATE TEACHERS

(College) Valsire Philips

MUSICAL GROUPS

"I started fast in Elementary School moving to Advanced Band because there were only two tuba players in all ten elementary schools. Jr. and Sr. High Honor Bands and orchestras. First chair in Northern California Honor Band."

College bands
"Marching Band. Organized and led Homecoming Band Days (for high school bands – four years)"
Humboldt State Univ. "Pirates of Penzance"
Humboldt Light Opera Company
Rogue Valley Symphony 1976-77
Rogue Community Theater "Oklahoma," "South Pacific," "Annie," "Carrousel," "Camelot," "Music Man"
Escorted church youth groups on singing tours 1982, 1983
Siskiyou College Orchestra 1986 –
Redding, Calif. Symphony 1988 –
Shasta, Calif. Symphony 1993 –
Southern Oregon Symphonic Band 1994 –
Marching Male Chauvinist Pigs Eureka, Calif. (Cymbals) Parades along West Coast 1975-78

OCCUPATION - PROFESSION
Band instrument repair

HONORS AND AWARDS
John Philip Sousa Award, 1967
Who's Who in American Universities, 1971
Owen Hayes Award for Outstanding Cymbal Player. Eureka, Calif.

AT HOME: Medford, Ore.

Kent SMITH (Trumpet)
Born: (Carbondale, Ill.) Aug. 13, 1967
Married: Tionne 1987

EDUCATION
Ashland High School Grad. 1985
Southern Oregon State College, 1985-87

BEGAN STUDYING INSTRUMENTAL MUSIC
Colorado Springs, 1977 - Trumpet

MUSICAL GROUPS
Ashland High School Band
Southern Oregon Symphonic Band, 1994

OCCUPATION-PROFESSION
Produce manager - Super Market

AT HOME: Ashland, Ore.

Tionne SMITH (Flute)

Born: (New Brunswick, NJ) Jan 21, 1967
Married: Kent Smith, 1987

EDUCATION
Crater High School, Central Point, Ore. Grad. 1985
Southern Oregon State College, BS, Psychology, 1990

BEGAN STUDYING INSTRUMENTAL MUSIC
Flute - 5th grade

PRINCIPAL INSTRUMENTAL TEACHERS
Don Bieghler, 9 -12th grades - 1983-85

PRIVATE TEACHERS
Sheryl Kannasto - flute

MUSICAL GROUPS
Scenic Jr. High School Band
Crater High School Band
Southern Oregon State College Band
Southern Oregon Symphonic Band, 1994

OCCUPATION-PROFESSION
Senior Ass't Mgr., DJ's Video

AT HOME: Ashland, Ore.

Beverly SPJUT (Trumpet)

Born: (San Mateo, Calif.) Sept. 9, 1950

EDUCATION
Strandwood Elementary School
Pleasant Hill Intermediate School
College Park High School. Grad. 1968
Humboldt State Univ. Arcata, Calif. BS - Nursing. 1972

BEGAN STUDYING INSTRUMENTAL MUSIC
Strandwood Elementary School, Pleasant Hill, Calif, at 10 years old.
Mrs. Caldwell, teacher

PRINCIPAL INSTRUMENTAL TEACHERS
Strandwood Elementary School - Mrs. Caldwell
Pleasant Hill Intermediate School - Mr. Hodges
College Park High School - Mr. Ned Mortensen

PRIVATE TEACHERS
Red Gillum
Larry Hudson - Trumpet

Beverly Spjut started with a Bugle at a Camp Fire Girls summer camp later won the coveted John Phillip Sousa Award in school. Now she is a Trumpeter in Southern Oregon Symphonic Band.

MUSICAL GROUPS
Southern Oregon State College Band
Ashland City Band - (Raul Maddox. Cond.)
Humboldt State University Band and Brass Choir
Rogue Valley Brass Choir
Southern Oregon Symphonic Band, 1993 –

OCCUPATION - PROFESSIONS
Registered Nurse - Emergency Room
Mother - Homemaker

HONORS AND AWARDS
John Philip Sousa Band Award (Band Student of the Year) College Park High School, 1968
At age 12, was Official Bugler at Camp Fire Girls Summer Camp

AT HOME: Ashland, Ore. Two children – teens

→LEAVE OF ABSENCE

Leo STAN (B*b*-Clarinet)

Born: (Detroit, Mich.) Apr. 12, 1919
Married

EDUCATION
Cass Technical High School – Music
U. S. Navy School of Music, Washington, D.C.
Selmer: Musical Instrument Repairs (G.I. Bill)

BEGAN STUDYING INSTRUMENTAL MUSIC
Cass Technical High School - Reeds

PRINCIPAL INSTRUMENTAL TEACHERS
Rex Brandt; Robert Woods; Bill Berk ; George Post

PRIVATE TEACHERS
Rosser Detroit; Netting Detroit

MUSICAL GROUPS
Ashland City Band 2 years.
Hillah Temple Shrine German Band, Harry Kannasto, Dir.
ABC Band - Ashland, Ore.
Johnny Lampson Dance Band 15 years
Southern Oregon Symphonic Band 1 year

MILITARY SERVICE
U.S.Navy – Nov. 20, 1940 - Jan. 19, 1946
Naval Training Center, Great Lakes, Ill.
USS New York (Battleship)
USS Tennessee (Battleship)
USS South Dakota (Battleship)
USN D.D. Hunters Point, San Francisco, Calif.
Naval Training Center, Bainbridge, Md.,

OCCUPATION - PROFESSION
Sales and Merchandising - Seagram Distilleries
Trade Show Exhibitor
Musical Instrument Repair

HONORS AND AWARDS
Military Decorations:
Asiatic-Pacific Campaign Medal with 5 Battle Stars, American Defense Medal, American Theater Medal, Victory Medal, Navy Unit Commendation Citation "Heroism against the Japanese [while aboard] *USS Tennessee,* " Philippine Liberation Medal

AT HOME: Ashland, Ore.

George W. STEPHEN (B*b*-Clarinet)
Born: (London, Eng.) Sept. 28, 1936

EDUCATION
St. Anselmo Grammer (Private), Southoll, Middlesex, Eng.

BEGAN STUDYING INSTRUMENTAL MUSIC
Private lessons at age 15
Royal Air Force College Affiliated London Royal Academy of Music –18 months, Middlesex, Eng.

MUSICAL GROUPS
Royal Air Force Far East Band and Dance Band.
Big Dance Bands (Professional) Eric Winston, Val Merral, Frank Wier, Teddy Foster (Baritone and Alto Saxophones)
George Stephen Modern Jazz Quartet – full-time Night Clubs 1963-64.
"I left the business in 1964 to study Yoga."
Southern Oregon Symphonic Band, 1992 –

MILITARY SERVICE
Royal Air Force Full-time bandsman. Duty stations: London; Singapore; Hong Kong; Philippine Isl.; Borneo; Malaya, 1956-58

OCCUPATION - PROFESSION
Business Owner: Tub and Tile Refinishing

HONORS & AWARDS
General Services Medal (British) for Malaya

AT HOME: Medford.

Neil STONE (Baritone Horn)
Born: (Portland, Ore.) Sept. 28, 1922

EDUCATION
Central Point Elementary and High School, Central Point, Ore. Grad. 1940
Southern Oregon State College

BEGAN STUDYING INSTRUMENTAL MUSIC
Trumpet - 6th Grade, Central Point Elementary School.
Trumpet - Central Point High School

PRINCIPAL INSTRUMENTAL TEACHERS
1938 - Mr. Botts, Central Point Elementary School
1938-41 Harry Meyers, Central Point High School
1941-45 Clyde C. Owens, Portland Army Air Base, Portland, Ore. and San Francisco, Calif.
1950-53 Glenn Matthews, Southern Oregon State College

Neil Stone in
Band uniform of
Southern Oregon
State College
about 1950

PRIVATE TEACHERS
Hattie Core
Wilson Waite

MUSICAL GROUPS
Portland Army Air Base Band, Portland, Ore.
Army Service Forces Band, San Francisco, Calif
D.A.V. Band, Klamath Falls, Ore. 1950
Klamath Falls City Band, 1950
Southern Oregon College Band, 1950-53
Elks Band, Astoria, Ore. 1953-55
Ashland City Band, Ore. 1957-60
Southern Oregon Symphony Orchestra, 1957-609
Hillah Temple Shrine Band, 1958-60; 1969-72
Hartness Eve Band, Salinas, Calif. 1962-67
Southern Oregon Symphonic Band, 1990 –
<u>Director:</u>
Lewis and Clark College Conservatory No. 5 Band, 1953-55
Boy Scout Band, Astoria, Ore. 1954-55
Rogue River High School Band and Chorus, Rogue River, Ore. 1955-60.
Rogue River Elementary Bank 1955-60
Shasta County Band, Redding, Calif., 1960-61
Soledad Elementary Band, Soledad, Calif., 1961-68
Soledad Correctional Facility Band, Soledad, Calif., 1963-64
Gonzales High School Band, Gonzales, Calif. (Summer 1966)
Elkton High School - Elementary Bands and Chorus, Elkton, Ore., 1968-69.
Prospect High School - Elementary Bands and Chorus, Prospect, Ore., 1970-71
Soledad Elementary Scholl Band, Soledad, Calif., 1972-77
Soledad Mission Elementary School Band, 1973-77
Junction Elementary School Bands, Palo Cedro, Calif., 1977-79
Soledad Elementary Bands and Chorus, 1979-80

MILITARY SERVICE
March 3, 1941 - July 18, 1945
586 Army Air Force Band
457 Army Service Forces Band

OCCUPATION - PROFESSION
Instrumental Music Teacher - Retired 1980

AT HOME: Medford, Ore.

John E. STOWE (Trombone)
Born: (Niles, Mich.) Sept, 28, 1927
Married: Melissa Mott (1993)

EDUCATION
Penrose High School Grad. 1945
Univ. of Colorado, BA. 1951; M.Ed. 1953

BEGAN STUDYING INSTRUMENTAL MUSIC
Fort Lewis, Wash. 1946.

PRINCIPAL INSTRUMENTAL TEACHERS
Hugh McMillen, Univ. of Colorado

MUSICAL GROUPS
U. S. Army, various bands at Fort Lewis, Wash., Truax AFB, Madison, Wisc.
Slide Effects Troubadour Brass
Rogue Valley Wind Ensemble
Brass Group Ensemble/Rogue Valley English Hand Bell Festival
Southern Oregon Symphonic Band Charter Member

MILITARY SERVICE
U. S. Army - 1945-47
U. S. Air Force - 1952-53

OCCUPATION - PROFESSION
Music Instrument Repair Technician
Taught Instrumental Music then became Principal US Air Force Academy Schools, Colorado, 1959-1974

HONORS AND AWARDS
French Unit Citation for Valor (2nd Infantry)
Elected President of Eastern Div. of Classroom Teachers, State of Colorado

AT HOME: Medford. Four children – grown

Melisa Stowe, earlier (left), then during Concert at V.A. Domiciliary Sept. 24, 1994

Melissa STOWE (French Horn)

Born: (Framingham, Mass.) June 7, 1947

Married: John (1993)

EDUCATION

East Brunswick High School, N.J. Grad. 1965

Indiana University 1970-73 in Alternative Education. Completed study in Early Childhood Educ., Wanbonsee College, Sugar Grove, Ill.

BEGAN STUDYING INSTRUMENTAL MUSIC

Exeter, New Hampshire, 6th Grade (Mellophone)

East Brunswick High School. (Fr. Horn)

PRINCIPLE INSTRUMENTAL TEACHERS

Jerry Kupchinsky, Orchestra – East Brunswick High School.

Bob Weiler and Mario DeCarolas, Band – East Brunswick High School Band

PRIVATE TEACHERS

Richard Gerstenberger, Rutgers Univ.

MUSICAL GROUP

East Brunswick High School bands and orchestras

New Jersey All State Band as sophomore.

Middlesex County Orchestra

Princeton Community Summer Band
Southern Oregon State College Symphonic Band, Max McKee, Cindy Huftion
State of Jefferson Sometimes Marching Band
Ashland City Band, Raoul Maddox.
Rogue Valley Wind Ensemble, Bill Norfleet
Rogue Valley Symphony, Art Shaw
Rogue Community College Chamber Orchestra, Jim Rich
Rogue Valley Brass Ensemble, Dr. Marvin Belford
Brass Group Ensemble/Rogue Valley English Hand Bell Festival
Southern Oregon Symphonic Band, 1991 –

OCCUPATION AND PROFESSION
Teacher (Head Start): Early Childhood Development
Musical Instrument Repair technician
Worked with emotionally disturbed children in Ill. and Ore.

AT HOME: Medford, Ore. Four children (previous marriage) – grown

---

Laurence C. "Larry" WARE DMD (Bass Clarinet)
Born: (Corvallis, Ore.) Nov. 14, 1934
Married: Loretta (1955)

EDUCATION
Corvallis High School, Corvallis, Ore. 1952
Oregon State College BS 1956
University of Oregon Dental School DMD, 1959

BEGAN STUDYING INSTRUMENTAL MUSIC
Freshman though Sophomore Years in High School (Clarinet)

MUSICAL GROUPS
Hillah Temple Shrine Band 1980 –
Hillah Temple German Band
Rogue Valley Wind Ensemble
Southern Oregon Symphonic Band Charter Member

OCCUPATION - PROFESSION
Dentist

AT HOME: Medford, Ore. Three children – grown

Bert Webber (above) when with Seattle Elks Band in 1957. Now, 1994 (right), plays with the Southern Oregon Symphonic Band

Ebbert T. "Bert" WEBBER (Baritone Horn)

Born: (Maryland) Oct 22, 1921

Married: Marjorie Jean "Margie" Renfroe. BS. (RN -ret) 1944

EDUCATION

Geo. Washington High School - San Francisco, Calif. - Grad. 1940
Univ. of Nevada (Reno) Preflight aviation #313th CTD (Air Force) 1943
Paramount Studios, NY. Sig. Corps Newsreel Cameraman - Cert. 1944
National Sales Training Inst. - New York - Cert. 1956
Whitworth College (Spokane) - BA Journalism/Library Science/Educ. 1965
Portland State Univ. Grad. School, Library Science - 1967
Univ. of Portland - Master Degree/Library Science - 1968

BEGAN STUDYING INSTRUMENTAL MUSIC

Presidio Jr. High School - Trumpet/Baritone - San Francisco 1934-37
Geo. Washington High School - Baritone - San Francisco 1938-40

PRINCIPAL INSTRUMENTAL TEACHERS

Martin A. Pihl (Jr. High School) Marion Knott, (Sr. High School)
Chesley M. Mills (prev. cond. San Diego Symphony)

Mr. Mills was hired by *The San Francisco News* to direct the *News* Carrier's Band and to offer free (Depression years) private lessons to those who wished them.

PRIVATE TEACHERS

Chesley M. Mills - San Francisco 1937-40.

MUSICAL GROUPS

Geo. Washington High School R.O.T.C. Band - (Baritone)

San Francisco News Carriers Band, San Francisco, 1936-40

Kodiak, Alaska 1942 - 215th Coast Artillery Band (Guest) - (Baritone)

Reno. Univ of Nevada. Summer 1943. Recruited military band from Air Force Aviation Cadet unit (#313th CTD) parades, light concert. (Director)

Santa Ana Army AFB Flight No. 1 Band. Winter 1943 (Baritone)

Sedro-Woolley, Wash. 1953-55. American Legion Clown Band. Parades and light concert. (Baritone, Valve Trombone - Director)

Seattle, Wash. 1956-58. Seattle Elks Band. (Baritone - Rehearsal Cond.)

Seattle, Wash. 1958. Shrine Band. (Baritone)

Taught "Bugling" Boy Scout Merit Badge, Camp Cowles Scout Reservation, Newport Wash. Organized new Bugle Corps with new boys for performance each week for 8-week summer camp period, 1965-66. Organized and Directed Drum & Bugle Corps for World Scout Jamboree, Farragut, Idaho, 1967.

Southern Oregon Symphonic Band. 1993 –

MILITARY SERVICE (Years: 5+)

Regular U.S. Army 1940-45. Alaska, Scotland, England, France, Belgium. Signal Corps telephone service, installation & maintenance; Air Force Pilot School Santa Ana AFB - Tex Rankin Academy, Tulare; Minter Field, Bakersfield, Calif.; Returned to Signal Corps as Cameraman and photo-lab specialist & Motion Picture Cameraman.

OCCUPATION - PROFESSION

Salesman age 9, *The Sat. Eve Post* –. Owner WEBBER PHOTO SUPPLY CO. and Commercial Photographer (Sedro Woolley, Wash.) 1945-55. Remington Office Machine sales (Seattle, Lewiston, Spokane) 1955-61. Chief of Photo Services, Whitworth College, 1962-65; Teacher-Librarian Jr /Sr High 1965-70: Author, over 50 non-fiction books. 1973 –. Research Photo-journalist; book publisher, editor. Owns: WEBB RESEARCH GROUP PUBLISHERS; REFLECTED IMAGES PUBLISHERS; PACIFIC NORTHWEST BOOKS

HONORS AND AWARDS

Tangley-Oakes Graduate Fellowship in Library Science 1968

Honorary Life Membership, Friends of Old Fort Stevens 1976

Listed in *Who's Who in the West; Who's Who in the World; Contemporary Authors; Oregon Authors; International Biographical Center* (Cambridge, Eng.).

Military Decorations: American Defense Medal with pre-war Foreign Service Star; American Theater Service Medal; Asiatic-Pacific Service Medal; European-African-Middle-Eastern Service Medal; Good Conduct Medal; Victory Medal; Presidential Unit Citation; Official U. S. Army Signal Corps Photographer patch.

AT HOME: Central Point, Ore. (1969) Four children –grown

Virginia Westerfield as Director of the Band at Rogue River High School.

Virginia WESTERFIELD (B♭ Clarinet)

Born: (Ashland, Ore.) Mar. 21, 1919

Widow

EDUCATION

Medford High School, Medford, Ore. Grad. 1937

Southern Oregon State College (twice - returned 1951-52)

San Francisco State Teacher's Band Course

Innumerable summer schools and music workshops

"I lived in a band studio so learned to transpose, arrange and fingering of various brass instruments while still in high school."

BEGAN STUDYING INSTRUMENTAL MUSIC

"In 1933, my new stepdad, Steve Whipple, from the Olmstead Band Studio, San Jose, started me on Soprano Saxophone then he taught me the Clarinet with which I went into the high school band. "

PRINCIPAL INSTRUMENTAL TEACHERS

Wilson Waite, Medford High School Band/Orchestra

Lucie Landon, Southern Oregon State College Orchestra

Lee Chrisman, San Francisco State Teachers Band Specialist

Max McKee, Southern Oregon State College Band

Clarence Sawhill, Siskiyou Band Camp

PRIVATE TEACHERS

Lucie Landon, Violin

Steve Whipple

MUSICAL GROUPS

"The Steve Whipple Junior Band, Medford, ages 4th grade through High School, was the Medford area civic effort at having a Band for parades, etc. This was before much organized instrumental music in the schools. Was made up primarily of 7th and 8th graders. Steve's "students" met in his studio for after school instructions and practice. *These were the best years of my life and all before TV.* It was a great time. I have been playing for dances since I was 16.

" I played with professional dance band, "The Music Makers" until World War II took some of the men, then I filled in with other bands. Played Alto Sax all over Southern Oregon with all-girls dance band, "The Harmony Honeys." Led a jazz group that had a continuing gig every Saturday night at Medford Dreamland Ballroom for a couple of years. Played several years with Jimmy Skillen's big dance band in Medford. It finally broke up in 1994. Played with many Dixieland groups. About 1960, I organized and directed the Salvation Army Junior Band for one year."

Rogue Valley Philharmonic Orchestra, Richard Werner (1950's)

Ashland City Band, Many directors including Irv Mirick, Herb Cecil, Raoul Maddox, Dave Wight; guest conductors Warren Barker, James de Priest (from high school to the present time)

91st Division Artillery Band (Camp White, Ore.) WO David McGregor 1942. "I practiced with them and played in two concerts as guest Alto Saxophone soloist; also played in Clarinet section."

Jack Teagarden's Dance Orchestra, 1945. "Jack's 3rd Alto Sax player was ill and on leave. I was hired to sit in"

Southern Oregon State College Band, Mac McKee 1979 –

Southern Oregon Wind Ensemble

The State of Jefferson Sometimes Marching Band

Southern Oregon State College Alumni Band

The Band Director's Band of Western International Band Clinic, Les Brown, Tim Lotsenheiser, Max McKee

The Director's Band of the ABC Band College (SOSC), 1989 –

Directors included: Frank Bencriscutto (Michigan State Univ. Bands); Jan de Mys (The Netherlands); Phillippe Langlet (France); Randall Spicer, Jan Chattaway, Alfred Redd, John Paynter, Col. Arnold Gabriel, USAF Ret., Clare Grundman, etc.

Hillah Temple German Band , 1994 –

Southern Oregon Symphonic Band, 1993 –

OCCUPATION-PROFESSION

Musician and Free Lance Writer

"I was a public school instrumental music teacher (had the Rogue River High School Band, Orchestra, Choir, 9 years) then after 12 years in old Medford School District 49C, giving technique lessons in the Jr. and Sr high schools, and had a grade school band most years, retired in 1964.

"I came out of retirement in 1993 and am teaching Ashland Middle School Band program under *aegis* of the Foster Grandparent Program. I am coaching woodwinds in eight bands by ones and twos, and I also get worked in to brass and percussion."

HONORS AND AWARDS

"My last two years in high school, I won the Oregon State Championship Saxophone medals at payoffs in Eugene and Corvallis. Subsequently, my picture was in the *CONN Music Magazine* "Hall of Fame" for student musicians."

AT HOME: Ashland, Ore. One child - grown

Margaret WILSON (B♭-Clarinet)

Born: (Eugene, Ore.) Feb. 6, 1940
Married: Jerry Wilson (1959)

EDUCATION
Pleasant Hill High School, Pleasant Hill, Ore. Grad. 1957

BEGAN STUDYING INSTRUMENTAL MUSIC
Clarinet, 7th grade

PRINCIPAL INSTRUMENTAL TEACHERS
Arnold Martin, Band teacher, Pleasant Hill, Ore. 1951-57

PRIVATE TEACHERS
Arnold Martin

MUSICAL GROUPS
Ashland City Band 1961-64
Southern Oregon Symphonic Band 1993 –

OCCUPATION - PROFESSION
Women's Bible Study Teacher – Bible Study Fellowship (International) 1971-81
Woman's Bible Study (Independent) 1992–

AT HOME: Medford, Ore. Two children – grown

Band Directors of the Hillah Temple Shrine Band and the Southern Oregon Symphonic Band – 1909 - 1994

The Hillah Temple Shrine Band was founded in 1909, Shriner E. A. Shepard, Director. The research committee was unable to determine the identities of Directors after Mr. Shepard until Ward Croft sometime just before the start of World War-II.

The Shrine Band (1909) is the "grandfather" band of the Southern Oregon Symphonic Band which was founded February 25, 1987. The "father" of the present band was the Southern Oregon Men's Symphonic Band.

Previous directors: Ward Croft, Harry Meyers, Henry Enders, Charles Cook, Irving A. Mirick, Raoul Maddox, Charles Mason.

Harry Kannasto is the present Director of the Shrine Band.

John E. Drysdale is the present Director of the Southern Oregon Symphonic Band.

Harvey C. WOODS DMD (Baritone Horn/Trumpet)

Born: (Ashland, Ore.) May 12, 1935

Married: Janet (1965)

EDUCATION

Ashland High School, Grad. 1953
University of Oregon, BA General Science
Oregon Health Sciences Center Dental School, DMD 1964

BEGAN STUDYING INSTRUMENTAL MUSIC

Elementary School. Ervin Lesser, teacher

PRINCIPAL INSTRUMENTAL TEACHERS

Classroom teachers

MUSICAL GROUPS

Grade school and high school bands and ensembles
Ashland City Band, 1952-58 (Trumpet)
University of Oregon Marching Band, 1954 - Dr. Ira Lee
University of Oregon Concert Band 1953-54 - Dr. Robert Wagner
Hillah Temple Shrine Band (part-time) 1953-54; 1964 –
Ashland City Band, (Trumpet and Baritone Horn) 1984 –
Hillah Temple German Band, 1964–
Southern Oregon Symphonic Band Charter Member

MILITARY SERVICE

U.S. Army - 1958-60 Dental Ass't at Valley Forge Gen. Hospital, Phoenixville, Pa.

OCCUPATION - PROFESSION

Dentist

AT HOME: Medford. Three children – grown

Index

Page numbers printed in ***bold italic*** type are photographs